ANIMAL ACTION ANNUAL 2009

THIS BOOK BELONGS TO

Ruby

First published in Great Britain by Think Books in 2008
This edition published in 2008 by Think Books, an imprint of Pan Macmillan Ltd
Pan Macmillan, 20 New Wharf Road, London N1 9RR, Basingstoke and Oxford
Associated companies throughout the world
www.panmacmillan.com
www.think-books.com

ISBN: 978-1-84525-067-6
Text ©: Pan Macmillan Ltd, RSPCA, Think Publishing
Design ©: RSPCA and Think Publishing

Editor: Sarah Evans
Designer: Lou Millward
For Think Books: Tania Adams, Camilla Doodson, Richard Rees, Dom Scott, Marion Thompson, Shelley Varley
For RSPCA: Damion Diplock, Rachel Fallone, Sarah Johnson, Becky Murray, Louise Stevens

1 3 5 7 9 8 6 4 2 1

A CIP catalogue record for this book is available from the British Library.

Printed and bound in Italy by L.E.G.O. S.p.A

Visit www.panmacmillan.com to read more about all our books and to buy them. You will also find features, author interviews and news of any author events, and you can sign up for e-newsletters so that you're always first to hear about our new releases.

Cover images
Kitten: Alan Robinson/RSPCA Photolibrary
Labrador puppy: Photolibrary.com

contents

contents

Welcome!

Hi, and welcome to the first ever *Animal Action* annual! Just like *Animal Action* magazine, it's packed with brilliant animal stories, fun and games, animal hospital diaries, creature features and fact files, celebrity animal chat, craft pages, posters and lots more!

The *Animal Action* team has pulled together all your favourite bits of the magazine - and lots of extras - to make this fabulous annual. So you get your favourite animal magazine, just much bigger - what could be better than that?

Get up close and personal with the residents of the RSPCA's donkey centre and, if you're thinking about working for the RSPCA, we've got it covered - there's advice on how to become an animal collection officer and a veterinary nurse, and where to find out about other jobs with the RSPCA.

And if you would like to become an RSPCA inspector, you can read all about how tough, but rewarding, the inspectors' training course is. It's a great job and lots of people want to be an RSPCA inspector so they can work for the biggest, most famous animal welfare organisation in the whole world!

I've had loads of fun working on the *Animal Action* annual, and I know you're going to enjoy all the fascinating facts, fantastic features and great puzzles.

If you like animals, you'll love the *Animal Action* annual.

Sarah

Sarah Evans, editor (and Coco!)

The RSPCA - then and now

It's amazing how the RSPCA has grown over the years - we haven't always been such a big organisation!

The first animal welfare organisation in the world

It all began one summer's evening more than 180 years ago. On 16 June 1824 a London vicar, the Reverend Arthur Broome, held a meeting at Old Slaughter's Coffee House to talk about setting up a society to stop people being cruel to animals.

Also at the meeting were the MPs (Members of Parliament) William Wilberforce, who is well-known for his campaign to end slavery, and Richard Martin (also known as 'Humanity Dick'), who was one of those responsible for the first law against cruelty to animals.

That evening the first national animal welfare organisation in the world was born – the Society for the Prevention of Cruelty to Animals (SPCA).

Changing attitudes

At that time, anyone with sympathy for animals was considered odd. Most people thought of animals as little more than 'things' that provided food, transport or sport.

In its early years the Society had to win over the hearts and minds of the general public – to change people's indifference to animal cruelty.

Our inspectors

The Society soon took on inspectors, who investigated animal cruelty and brought people to court. As the Society grew, our inspectors were issued with uniforms to give them more authority in the eyes of the public.

Amazingly, we began our investigative work five years before the first modern police force – the London Metropolitan Police.

By 1841 there were just five full-time inspectors. Today there are 323, plus 146 animal collection officers in England and Wales, and in 2007 our inspectors investigated 137,245 animal cruelty complaints.

Royal approval

By 1840 the Society's work was held in such high regard that Queen Victoria gave her permission for the SPCA to be called the Royal Society for the Prevention of Cruelty to Animals.

Modern times

Today, the Society still carries out the four-part action plan agreed in 1824. This was designed to help the public understand the needs of animals and to make sure people don't break animal welfare laws.

This is the action plan:
- To produce information on what animals need and how to care for them.
- To produce educational material for schools.
- To make appeals to the public in the press about cases of animal cruelty and neglect.
- To employ inspectors to check the condition of animals and prosecute people who cause animals to suffer.

We have 175 local branches with caring staff that work round-the-clock to help thousands of pets and wild animals at their animal centres and clinics. RSPCA staff and volunteers rehome about 70,000 unwanted or neglected pets every year! We also work to help farm animals and animals used in experiments.

Looking to the future

In 2007 a brilliant law came into force in the UK, called the Animal Welfare Act. This means that inspectors can take action a lot earlier than they could before if they believe an owner isn't caring for their animal properly. Before this Act they had to wait until the animal was actually suffering. This new law means that we can help many, many animals before they suffer.

We do lots of great things at the RSPCA, and it's all to help animals in some way.

FUN & GAMES

WORDSEARCH

In this wordsearch we're looking at a group of amazing predators that mostly hunt at night – owls! They may appear forwards, backwards, up, down or diagonally.

BARN ✓
TAWNY ✓
LITTLE ✓
EAGLE ✓
ELF ✓
SNOWY ✓
SPECTACLED ✓
GREAT GREY ✓
LONG-EARED ✓
SHORT-EARED ✓
SPOTTED ✓
GREAT HORNED ✓

```
L N D A R S O E L F E L
D E L T T I L T V W H O
E D I C I G S A I B U N
L E E Y E R G T A E R G
G R T E H T M R K M M E
A A I N P O N D Y A S A
E E D P G G E L W N I R
O T P N E T H O O A T E
G R E A T H O R N E D D
T O E O O Y E R S G E V
L H P D N E R Y N W A T
O S P E C T A C L E D W
```

Whooooo's missing?

Each owl appears four times in the grid except one, which only appears three times. Can you spot which owl has flown off?

Odd one out

CAN YOU SPOT WHICH IS THE ODD ONE OUT, AND WHY?

It's not a mammal

FOX

DORMOUSE

TORTOISE

HEDGEHOG

ANSWERS ON PAGE 94

Behind the scenes at an RSPCA hospital

Two days – in winter and summer – in the life of RSPCA Greater Manchester Animal Hospital veterinary surgeon Steve Kirby.

A WINTER'S DAY

8am Winter has arrived and the mornings are now dark and cold. I arrive at work and check all the animal patients before starting the day's surgery.

9am When on surgery duty the first task of the day is to perform all the neutering operations – castrations (for males) and spays (for females). These operations prevent animals from breeding, which means fewer unwanted young. Sadly, every year hundreds of young animals end up homeless and mistreated because of unwanted breeding. When buying a pet, getting the animal neutered should be classed as a necessity, along with vaccination and regular worming.

12pm A five-week-old kestrel called Kes is brought in because her owner has noticed a lump on the side of her head. We carefully anaesthetise the bird, which allows us to take a closer look, and discover an abscess in her outer ear. I delicately remove the abscess before Kes is woken up and kept warm while she recovers from the operation.

Birds of prey do not make good pets – they need professional care and owners must have expert knowledge to be able to look after them properly.

2pm My lunch is cut short when one of the inspectors rushes in with a collapsed cat, found abandoned in an empty house. A thorough clinical examination reveals he is hypothermic – this is when the animal's body temperature becomes too low. We warm him up slowly on a heat mat and give him warm fluids through a drip. Hopefully, with careful nursing, he will make a full recovery and be successfully rehomed.

3.30pm My final job of the day is to examine a tortoise called Eric that has started to wake up from hibernation. If tortoises are not kept at the right temperature through the winter, they can wake up. This can kill the tortoise if not spotted because it won't have enough food stored in its body to keep it alive.

I measure and weigh Eric – he's underweight and too ill to hibernate this year. He needs careful feeding and regular health checks to survive the winter. Many tortoises die every year because they are not given the right conditions for hibernation. Tortoises also need to be looked after carefully by people who know what they are doing and can provide the right facilities – they don't make suitable pets.

4.30pm I've just enough time to have a final look at all the patients. Kes has recovered well and is ready to go home, and the stray cat is responding to treatment and seems much happier in the warmth!

A SUMMER'S DAY

8am Summer can be a busy time for the hospital and there's already a queue forming outside. My first client is a cat called Jasmine. Her owner says she's been losing hair and has developed scabs along her back – a classic sign of a flea allergy. Jasmine needs a course of antibiotics and monthly flea treatment.

9am A young pet rabbit is brought in that is sluggish and not eating. An examination reveals the problem – fly strike. Blow flies lay eggs in the matted fur around the rabbit's hindquarters and the eggs develop into maggots, which feed off the rabbit. It's a horrible situation. The affected area is clipped and cleaned thoroughly. Rabbits need regular checks for fly strike during the warmer months.

11am An elderly lady brings in her beloved white cat Sampson. She has noticed that the tips of his ears have become very red. Sampson loves lying in the sun and I suspect this is sunburn. Sampson needs antiseptic ointment and must stay out of direct sunlight. It's important to apply a high-factor sunscreen to exposed areas of skin, especially for white animals that enjoy the sun.

2pm After lunch a man rushes in with his Staffordshire bull terrier. The dog seems very distressed and is retching and pawing at his mouth. The owner thinks he may have swallowed a bone at a family barbecue. I can't see anything so I send the dog for an X-ray, which shows a bone lodged in his throat.

An endoscope (a tube with a camera on the end) lets me see down his throat and I am able to remove the bone. This situation could have been fatal if the bone hadn't been removed quickly.

3.30pm Another emergency is brought straight through. A small Jack Russell terrier has been found collapsed on the back seat of his owner's car. He is panting heavily and is very hot. The little dog is probably suffering from severe heat stroke and needs to be cooled down quickly using intravenous fluids and cool, damp flannels.

Every year dozens of dogs die from overheating in hot weather. Dogs can't sweat like people so water should always be available to help them cool down. During these hot spells animals should not be left in cars – even for a short time.

4.30pm There's just enough time to check the in-patients with the emergency night vet before I go. Hopefully the evening will be quiet, but the hot weather is bound to bring in some unusual cases.

Pick-a

During the colder months, birds may have trouble finding food and water. You can help by making sure they have something delicious to eat and drink every day.

- It's very important to feed birds but please try to remember to keep filling the bird bath with fresh water when temperatures fall below freezing. If possible, do it twice a day – first thing in the morning and again mid-afternoon, well before it gets dark.

- Check that all feeders and food are in a safe place, away from cats and squirrels, and move bird tables daily to prevent a build up of dropped food, which may lead to disease.

- Please also ensure that all feeders, water bowls and bird tables are cleaned daily and scrubbed with a mild disinfectant weekly.

- Don't forget to wear rubber gloves.

- Birds also like cheese, nuts, stale cake crumbs and dried fruit.

WHAT YOU NEED

- Empty drinks carton
- Ruler
- Pencil
- Scissors
- String
- Wood for perch
- Empty yoghurt pots
- Lard
- Birdseed
- Saucepan
- Wooden spoon
- Pine cones
- Peanut butter

For a quick treat, smear peanut butter on to a pine cone, roll in birdseed and tie to a branch with string. Yummy!

For bird food try
CJ WildBird Foods Ltd
You can buy wild birdseed from CJ WildBird foods at: www.birdfood.co.uk, pet shops and some supermarkets and garden centres. CJ WildBird foods is a great supporter of the RSPCA.

...peck!

Instant feeder

1 Wash and dry an empty drinks carton. Using the photo and drawing as guides, use a ruler and pencil to draw a similar shape on the front and sides. Cut out the shape.

2 Staple the top together, if necessary. Punch two holes to thread a length of string through. Make a hole at the bottom of the feeder and poke a long length of dowel (small wooden rod) right through to act as a perch. Fill the feeder with birdseed and hang from a branch.

Special treat

1 For this bit you will need an adult's help. Put half the block of lard in a saucepan and heat it very gently until it melts. Add a breakfast cup of birdseed and remove from the heat. Stir well!

2 When the mixture has cooled a bit, spoon into empty yoghurt pots. Poke a length of string into the middle of the warm mixture. When set, carefully ease the fat ball out of the pot and hang on the branch of a tree. What a tweet!

Pet Care

THE RIGHT PET FOR YOU?

Dogs make very good companions, are intelligent, faithful and fun. But they take up a lot of time and energy, are quite expensive to look after and need plenty of space. A dog is not a good choice for people who are out all day. Typically, dogs live for about 13 years, so owning a dog is a big responsibility.

Dogs

WHAT DO DOGS NEED?

🐾 FOOD AND WATER

- A dog needs a well-balanced diet to stay fit and healthy.
- Provide your dog with access to clean, fresh drinking water at all times.
- Feed your dog at least once every day (unless advised otherwise by a vet).
- Adjust how much you feed your dog to make sure it doesn't become under or overweight.
- An individual's diet depends on its age, lifestyle, weight and health.
- Some human food (e.g. chocolate and onions) can be poisonous to dogs.

🐾 A GOOD HOME

- Make sure your dog's home is safe and secure.
- Provide your dog with a comfortable, dry, clean and quiet place to rest.
- Your dog needs regular access (at least every few hours) to an appropriate place where it can go to the toilet, otherwise it will become distressed.
- Your dog must have somewhere it can hide if it's frightened.
- Dogs need lots of space to exercise and regular opportunities to play.
  - Make sure your dog has suitable things to chew and play with.

- It is your responsibility to clean up your dog's faeces and dispose of it properly and responsibly.

🐾 COMPANY

- Dogs are sociable animals that need and enjoy company.
- If your dog is treated well as a puppy, it will see humans as friends.
- A dog may suffer if it doesn't have company for a period of time. They become bored and can howl and bark. Make sure your dog is never left alone long enough for it to become distressed.
- Your dog must have a responsible adult to look after it when you go on holiday.

🐾 TO BEHAVE NORMALLY

- Your family should choose a type and size of dog that is suited to you, your home and lifestyle. A dog's behaviour depends on its type, age and past experiences.
- A dog needs regular exercise and lots of opportunities to walk, run and play.
- Training your dog using rewards will help it to behave properly and make it easier to control. Never punish a dog as this could cause it pain and suffering. Good training can improve your dog's quality of life too.
- Provide safe toys for your dog and regular opportunities to play with people and other friendly dogs.
- Make sure your dog has enough to do so that it doesn't become distressed or bored.
- If your dog shows changes in its normal behaviour, develops unwanted habits, or shows signs of stress or fear, ask your vet for advice.

> Visit your local library or use the internet to find out more information on your specific pet.

⊕ TO BE HEALTHY

- Individual dogs and different breeds show signs of pain and suffering in different ways.
- Check your dog for injury or illness every day, and take it to a vet for a health check at least once a year. If you suspect your dog is poorly, ask an adult to take it to a vet immediately.
- Ask your vet for advice on how you can protect your dog's health, such as vaccination, neutering and treatments to control parasites (e.g. fleas and worms).
- Keep your dog under control and don't let it stray.
- Have your dog neutered to avoid unwanted puppies. Neutering may also reduce roaming and mounting behaviour in male dogs.
- Carefully groom your dog regularly (ask your vet to show you how to brush your dog the right way), especially long-haired breeds.
- Help keep your dog's teeth healthy and keep up to date with regular veterinary dental checks.
- Have your dog microchipped in case it gets lost or stolen. Your dog should also wear a collar with its identification details.
- Never leave a dog in a car for any length of time, even with the window open.

Give animals a voice!

The RSPCA cares for and tries to protect all animals. There are laws in place to prevent people from being cruel to animals, but before these laws are made the RSPCA does lots of campaigning...

Here are four campaigns that the RSPCA worked on in 2008.

LAYING HENS

'Laying hens' are the hens that lay the eggs we eat – and there are 30 million reared in the UK every year! Sadly, most of them (19 million) are kept in horribly small cages known as 'battery cages'. These are made of wire and house four or five hens each and it's squashed and uncomfortable in there. In 2012 a law will come into force in Europe that will ban battery cages – but farmers will still be able to use 'enriched' cages that are hardly any better.

The RSPCA believes the only way to house laying hens is by giving them enough space to move around freely and stretch their wings, and litter to dustbathe in – something hens love to do and which is good for them.

ACTION

We can all help by only buying eggs with 'RSPCA Freedom Food', 'barn', 'free-range' or 'organic' written on the box. Or you can buy eggs at a free-range farm.

CHICKENS

Did you know that each year 850 million chickens are reared for their meat in the UK, and 90 per cent of them are not bred to higher welfare standards? You're not alone. Until the RSPCA joined forces with two celebrity chefs, Jamie Oliver and Hugh Fearnley-Whittingstall, at the beginning of 2008, people didn't really know just what terrible conditions the chickens were reared in.

The cheapest way for farmers to rear chickens is to fit as many chickens as they can in an area they can control – such as an enclosed shed – and encourage them to grow as quickly as possible.

● Each chicken has less space than the size of a telephone directory, which is even less room than poor egg-laying hens kept in battery cages.

● The chickens are bred to grow very quickly – many only live for 35 days.

This can cause them lots of health problems such as heart failure and lameness.

● The chickens are kept in dim light most of the time, which makes the birds less active, meaning they grow faster. They are only given a few hours of complete darkness each day to rest properly.

● These birds also have leg sores caused by contact with wood shavings on the floors of the sheds. These contain high levels of ammonia from the birds' poo and urine. Yuck!

ACTION

You can help by asking the adults in your house to only buy chicken that has been reared to higher welfare standards and is labelled 'Freedom Food', 'free-range' or 'organic'. These chickens will have been given lots of space, light, and 'enrichments' (toys to prevent boredom) to give them a happier, healthier life. For more information please visit: **www.rspca.org.uk**

PUPPY TRAFFICKING

If you and your family have made the huge decision to have a puppy, don't let anything spoil the magical moment when you take your new best friend home.

Evidence shows there's a busy trade in puppy trafficking between the Republic of Ireland and the UK, meaning vans full of puppies are ending up for sale in the UK. The laws that regulate puppy breeding in the UK don't apply to the Republic of Ireland, so farms have up to 1,000 breeding bitches not covered by any law.

When dishonest puppy breeders breed too often from bitches that are tired and sick, the newborn puppies can be underweight, carry disease, and have physical and psychological problems. These puppy farms often don't have enough staff, resulting in dark, dirty and very unhygienic places – the perfect conditions for nasty canine diseases to spread. Once they have taken delivery of the puppies, dishonest traders use newspaper adverts, the internet and some pet shops to sell the animals to innocent buyers.

ACTION

Please follow these simple rules if you are looking for a puppy.

● You should see a puppy with its mother in the place where it was bred. Ideally you should see the father too (or at least a photo of him). If you can't, you should be suspicious. Get as much information as possible about where the puppy has come from and beware if the breeder is from outside the UK.

● If you are told the puppy has been vaccinated, ask to see the vaccination card. Vaccination cards are easy to fake, so if the vet's contact details are not visible or have an address from outside the UK, it may not be genuine.

● Pedigree certificates are never a guarantee of the condition of a puppy. Unless they are for Kennel Club registered puppies, they may not even mean you are being sold a pure breed.

● Don't ever buy from someone who offers to deliver your puppy or arranges to meet you somewhere.

● Never buy a puppy just because you feel sorry for it. If you are concerned about the health or welfare of a puppy, please contact the RSPCA's cruelty line on: 0300 1234 999.

FIREWORKS

Every year more and more fireworks are being used to celebrate festivals, events and private parties. Fireworks can frighten any kind of animal but, according to research, dogs are the most scared of fireworks by far.

ACTION

The following tips may help your pet during the firework season.

- At the first sign of fireworks, close all windows and curtains and put on some music or the TV to mask and muffle the fireworks sounds.
- If your dog or cat shows any signs of fear, try to ignore his/her behaviour unless they are in danger – for example, if he/she is likely to harm themselves.
- Never show anger to your dog or cat if he/she appears frightened – this will only convince your pet that there really is something to be afraid of!
- Make sure your dog or cat is kept in a safe and secure environment at all times, so that he/she can't bolt and escape in reaction to

The RSPCA is backing *Sounds Scary!* a sound therapy CD containing lots of different loud noises, to play to your dog and gradually introduce it to loud noises in the lead-up to the firework season. For more information and to buy a copy of the CD go to: www.rspca.org.uk/fireworks

You can text*: **BANG** to **60022** for more tips on how to look after your pet during the fireworks season.

Check out: www.giveanimalsavoice.org.uk

*Texts cost provider's usual rate.

a sudden noise. If you have had your pet microchipped he/she is more likely to be returned safely.

- Try to attend an organised public display rather than holding your own. Organised displays are usually well publicised, which means that pet owners can prepare in advance.
- Keep cats and dogs indoors while any bonfire is alight.
  - Ensure that any bonfire is a safe distance from aviaries or rabbit/guinea pig accommodation.
  - Bonfires can be fatal for wild animals such as hedgehogs, which often crawl into them to sleep.
    - Build bonfires as late as possible to reduce this risk and make sure you disturb the bonfire's foundations to give any wildlife a chance to escape before it is lit.

Dogs...

- Do not fuss over or try to reassure your dog when he/she is frightened. Set a good example and ignore the fireworks noise yourself – play with a toy to see if your dog wants to join in, but don't force him/her to play.

- Exercise your dog during daylight hours – never take him/her for a walk when fireworks are being let off.
- If you know of another dog that is not scared by noises and gets on well with your dog, keep the two together during firework evenings and it could help your dog to realise that there's no need to be afraid.

Cats...

- If possible, keep your cat indoors when fireworks are likely to be set off – remember to lock the cat flap once he/she is indoors.
- Make sure your cat has somewhere to hide if he/she wants to – for example inside a cupboard, under some furniture or in a quiet corner. Don't try and tempt him/her out, as this causes increased stress.

Small animals...

- Provide lots of extra bedding for your pets so that they have something to burrow in.
- Partly cover cages, pens and aviaries with blankets so that one area is well soundproofed, but make sure that your pet is still able to look out.

FUN & GAMES

Pondlife

Ponds are teeming with loads of wonderful wildlife. If you get the chance, use an underwater viewer (they are like upside down periscopes!) to take a look below the pond's surface and learn about some of these creatures. But make sure you're safe and you don't disturb the animals too much – always go with an adult and don't touch the creatures with your hands or remove them from their pond!

We've listed eight creatures you may find in a pond, four of them have legs and four don't – can you guess which is which?

FRESHWATER SHRIMP

POND SNAIL

DRAGONFLY

SWAN MUSSEL

WATER BOATMAN

PEA-SHELL COCKLE

RAMSHORN SNAIL

WATER MITE

WORDSEARCH

We're thinking about ponds, and observing all the wonderful creatures that can be found in and around them.

For the wordsearch we've hidden 12 of these creatures in the grid. Can you find them all? They may appear forwards, backwards, up, down or diagonally.

- DRAGONFLY ✓
- FROG ✓
- KINGFISHER ✓
- WATER VOLE ✓
- HERON
- PONDSKATER ✓
- LEECH ✓
- FLATWORM ✓
- NEWT ✓
- WATER BOATMAN ✓
- POND SNAIL ✓
- WATER MITE

```
R E U P O N D S N A I L
L T R E H S I F G N I K
E F E M C O A L L Y W D
T R O B I E N A E F A R
P O N D S K A T E R T A
R G H R A M I W C A E G
C A M E T M B O H R R O
R I C X R O Y R U R V N
E E S E H O P M T O O F
O T T E D T N O T W L L
T A U M S G O I N V E Y
W A T E R B O A T M A N
```

MOFFI

MOFFI, YOU NEED **MORE** EXERCISE!

YOU'RE JUST **TOO** LAZY!

AS AN ENVIRONMENTALLY FRIENDLY DOG, I'M JUST TRYING TO **CONSERVE** ENERGY...

...FOR THE **PLANET,** OF COURSE!

ANSWERS ON PAGE 94

Hare

FACT FILE

● In the UK there are two types of hare - the brown hare and the mountain hare.

● Hares are larger than rabbits, with bigger ears and much longer legs that enable them to run up to 45 miles per hour.

● They live mostly in flat, open grassland and on farms that grow crops. These flat areas make it easier to detect approaching predators.

● The saying 'as mad as a March hare' comes from their behaviour in springtime when males and females seem to box with each other!

● Feeding, courtship and mating all take place after dark. But in summer, when the days are longer, hares become active before sunset and continue after sunrise.

● Female hares (called does) can have up to three litters a year and, on average, give birth to four young, called leverets. Thankfully, the hunting and coursing of hares with dogs was made illegal in 2005 when the Hunting Act was introduced.

FUN & GAMES

Riddle of the Swamp!

Can you solve the riddle to reveal a rather unpleasant insect that is often found around swamps?

My **FIRST** is in meal and chomp, but not in bite.

My **SECOND** is twice in the moon – I am very annoying at night.

My **THIRD** starts sting, but in itch it can't be found.

And my **FOURTH** starts quiet – I hardly make a sound.

My **FIFTH** is in USA, but not in Florida or Everglade.

My **SIXTH** is in sting and itch – if I bite that's how you'll pay.

My **SEVENTH** ends an insect – because that's what I am.

And my **LAST** is loud and clear in OUCH! Now try and swat me if you can!

WORDSEARCH

Imagine the grid below is a swamp. See if you can find 10 swamp creatures hidden in it. They may appear forwards, backwards, up, down or diagonally.

- ANACONDA
- CROCODILE ✓
- FIDDLER CRAB
- FLAMINGO ✓
- MOSQUITO
- MUDSKIPPER ✓
- PIRANHA
- RACOON ✓
- RAT ✓
- SCARLET IBIS

Ben's World

IF YOU COULD HAVE A RIDE IN A FLYING SAUCER, BEN, WHERE IN THE WHOLE UNIVERSE WOULD YOU CHOOSE TO VISIT?

BOURNEMOUTH!

©MIKE ORAM & JOHN PICKERING

BOURNEMOUTH! WOULDN'T YOU RATHER GO TO MARS OR VENUS OR TO SOME OTHER GALAXY?

NOPE. I LIKE BOURNEMOUTH, GORDON!

OH, COME ON, BEN, WHERE'S YOUR SENSE OF ADVENTURE?

OH, ALRIGHT THEN, BOURNEMOUTH IN WINTER!

ANSWERS ON PAGE 94

The right Stuff!

Animal Action joins a group of student inspectors and checks out the highs and lows of the Society's tough training course...

Any RSPCA inspector – whether based in the wilderness of north Wales or busy central London – could be called on to use a powerboat or abseil down a building or cliff to rescue a stranded animal. This means all trainee RSPCA inspectors have to learn about ropes and boats on their tough 12-month training course.

BOAT BASICS

Learning how to control a powerboat is only one of the boat skills an inspector needs. Trainee inspectors must also learn about charts (maps of the sea), tides, compass reading, anchoring, boat launching and boat beaching.

Trainees spend four days at an outdoor activities centre on the south coast, near Southampton, where they take a Royal Yachting Association course in powerboat handling. Two evenings are set aside for classroom study and the days are spent out on the water.

They share a variety of powerboats and learn how to control them. They're also given grid references and have to lead the rest of the group to a final destination, proving that they know how to read a compass and a chart.

NAVIGATIONAL SKILLS

Map and compass reading is a very important part of navigation.

Special instructors at the National Mountain Centre in north Wales teach inspectors navigation skills and how to abseil safely down the side of a cliff or building.

They begin with navigation. Everyone is given an Ordnance Survey map and a compass. By reading the map's contours (these are lines on the map that show how high the land is) and spotting landmarks, such as buildings and rivers, inspectors find their way through mist and rain in the Welsh countryside.

ROPE RESCUES

RSPCA inspectors rescue many animals and often need their rope training skills. Rope training could be used in lots of different situations – for example, if an animal is stuck half-way down a cliff, or has fallen down a well or disused mine shaft. Also, an inspector might have to rescue a dog abandoned on a balcony in a block of flats.

This part of the course can be the most frightening for the trainees because they have to walk backwards off a cliff using a variety of equipment.

MORE TO LEARN

Trainee inspectors also have to learn about lots more, including laws affecting animals, animal handling, taking statements from people and wildlife crime.

Head of learning and development, Chief Superintendent Brian Dalton said: "This isn't a fun week – it's a very serious part of the training course. The first thing they could be asked to do is rescue an animal using this equipment.

"Take a look at our website at www.rspca.org.uk and check out the brilliant work we do every day, helping animals in some way."

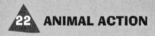

SO YOU WANT TO BE AN
RSPCA INSPECTOR

career corner

To find out about other careers with the RSPCA go to: www.rspca.org.uk/careers

THE JOB

An RSPCA inspector provides 24-hour cover for animals in need – investigating cruelty complaints, giving help and advice on animal care, carrying out rescues, inspecting animal establishments and bringing to court people who are cruel to an animal.

ENTRY REQUIREMENTS

Minimum of five GCSEs, minimum grade C (or equivalent), and experience of working with animals. You must be physically fit (able to swim 50m fully clothed) and hold a valid driving licence, but above all you must have excellent people skills.

TRAINING

Student inspectors must go on a challenging 12-month training course that teaches them about animal welfare law, investigation skills and interview techniques, court work, media and public speaking, mountain and boat rescue techniques, basic veterinary skills and animal-handling.

SO YOU WANT TO BE AN
ANIMAL COLLECTION OFFICER

THE JOB

When animals are injured, sick or need to be rescued from a threatening or dangerous location, an RSPCA animal collection officer (ACO) is often called in. ACOs must be able to deal with animals of every description and collect, secure and transport them safely and kindly. They have to put an animal to sleep when necessary and rescue animals (subject to training and certification of competence).

ENTRY REQUIREMENTS

Three GCSEs at A to C grade (English, maths and a science), and experience of working with animals is desirable. You must be in good physical health with a valid driving licence and experience of driving (animal collection officers do lots of driving!).

SO YOU WANT TO BE A
VETERINARY NURSE

THE JOB

RSPCA veterinary nurses are an important part of the veterinary team, providing expert nursing care for sick animals. The nurses work under the direction of a vet, carrying out diagnostic tests, minor surgical procedures and medical treatments. They also educate members of the public on how to keep their animals healthy and look after their welfare. The RSPCA employs small-animal veterinary nurses to work in their four small-animal hospitals. They mainly deal with cats, dogs and other small animals such as guinea pigs and hamsters. You could also train further to become an equine veterinary nurse.

ENTRY REQUIREMENTS

You must be at least 17 years old and have a minimum of five GCSEs at grade C or above or five Scottish standard grades 1 to 3. These must include English language, maths and a science subject.

TRAINING

Training is intensive and takes at least two years to complete. Most veterinary nurses train while they're working in an approved training practice, and will be continually assessed. They will also need to attend college.

There is also a degree and a Higher National Diploma (HND) course, both of which lead to registration as a veterinary nurse. These can take between three and four years.

How you can help...

If you're 16 or under, you can help the RSPCA in many ways! Here are a few ideas...

FAB FUNDRAISING

The first three letters in fundraising spell 'FUN'! So have a great time and raise money in aid of the RSPCA at the same time...

There are lots of different fundraising ideas – why not try a few of these?

- Bake cakes and biscuits and sell them to school friends.
- Set up a secondhand book and bric-a-brac stall.
- Sell off unwanted birthday and Christmas presents.
- Give up your favourite treats for a week and donate the money to the RSPCA.
- Grow plants and vegetables and sell them to family and friends.

SPONSORED STUFF

You can just about make up and do a sponsored anything! A sponsored skate-a-thon, sponsored silence, sponsored dog walk, sponsored knit, sponsored hula-hoop... the list is endless! So why not decide what you're going to do, then ask the RSPCA for a sponsorship form, and set a date to do it? Easy!

Phone: 0300 1234 555 for a form.

PEN POWER

You can also help the RSPCA by writing to your local MP (Member of Parliament) and questioning them on what they think about animal welfare issues.

The RSPCA is involved with all sorts of campaigns – from trying to stop real fur being used by fashion designers, to urging people to stop dropping litter because it could harm wildlife. Anyone can back RSPCA campaigns by writing, texting or e-mailing their local MP.

CAMPAIGN VOLUNTEERS

SPEAK OUT FOR ANIMALS

If you're dedicated to improving the lives of millions of animals, why not join the RSPCA's national campaigns network for ideas about how to campaign safely?

- Campaigners gather signatures, write letters, send e-mails, hold events, put up posters, deliver leaflets and contact the local press, generally spreading the message locally and rallying support.

- You can sign up online, or text* the word **JOIN** to **60022** to receive monthly e-mails or text messages letting you know how to get involved with RSPCA campaigns. As an RSPCA campaigner you'll receive free materials and giveaways to raise awareness of the campaigns in your area.

give animals a voice!

- Loads of young people have already signed up, and many are aged 12-15, so check out: **www.rspca.org.uk/campaigns** or e-mail: **campaigns@rspca.org.uk** for more details. *Texts cost your mobile provider's normal rate.

RAPID RECYCLE

Recycling is one of the easiest ways of raising money for the RSPCA, whether it's mobile phones, stamps or printer toner cartridges. All you have to do is phone the RSPCA (0300 1234 555) and ask for a recycling bag, then drop your item(s) in it and post it off – no stamp needed – or e-mail: rspcareturns@trf-uk.com

Odd one out

Can you spot the odd one out in each group?

COLOURS

chestnut   cob   dun   piebald

MARKINGS

sock   blaze   star   snip

TACK

bit   pommel   cantle   stirrup

FOOD

hay   bran   shavings   oats

FEET

frog   poll   wall   coronet

WORDSEARCH

As so many of you are pony mad, we've gone pony mad on these pages too! There's so much to discover about these beautiful animals. We've hidden 12 of them in the grid – can you find them all? They may appear forwards, backwards, up, down or diagonally.

- BAY
- BLUE ROAN
- BROWN
- CHESTNUT
- DAPPLE GREY
- DUN
- GREY
- IRON GREY
- LIVER CHESTNUT
- PIEBALD
- SKEWBALD
- STRAWBERRY ROAN

```
S H C H E S T N U T T Y E R G
T P Y D E A C R I C E A H A A
R U L O T R A O D L A B E I P
A D N Y E N Q F A K H G V D A
W T A T W T L D P S O N T I D
B T O O S X P U P L O Y T O F
E G R A Y E T Y L S E D A A E
R B E R M R H A E R S H S O F
R S U M O O S C G R E T K S G
Y M L W I Q H N R R C N E U I
R T B A J O O O E E Y L W V C
O R N P Z R P W Y K V N B B J
A U P U I B A E P T L I A W O
N A F Y K I D P F D R B L M Z
C L I V M R Y E A M R X D U N
```

GAMES

PONY PUZZLER

Solve the riddle and you'll name one of our best-known native breeds.

- My first is in small and saddle and shoes.
- My second is in hands and hay and hooves.
- My third is found three times in native breed.
- My fourth is in tack and tail and teeth.
- My fifth starts loose box, is in field but not in paddock.
- And my sixth is in Anglo and also in Arab.
- We're near the end now – not much more to say...
  My seventh is in bran and net but can't be found in hay.
- So to finish my name, another clue – just one more.
  My last is in donkey and dressage and Dartmoor!

Who am I?

TOP AND TAIL TRAIL

Can you fit the words into the trail? If you place them in the right order you'll find that the last letter of each word is the first letter of the next! We've got you started - you carry on!

**Roan Tail Gallop Numnah
Exmoor Saddle Trot Leg
Ponies Haynet**

Beat that!

In the equestrian world there are lots of different sports to get involved with. How many words of three letters or more can you find from

EQUESTRIAN?

1-40
Is that all? You haven't even left the stable yet!

41-65
You're barely trotting. Look a bit harder and break into a canter!

66-90
Much better. But if you gee up you're sure to find some more!

91+
Fantastic! You're a real champion!

We found **121!** Can you beat that?

ANSWERS ON PAGE 94

Pet Care

THE RIGHT PET FOR YOU?

Cats are very clean and make good companions for many people, but they can be quite expensive. Typically, cats live for about 14 years, but they can live much longer - therefore owning a cat is a big responsibility.

cats

Visit your local library or use the internet to find out more information on your specific pet.

WHAT DO CATS NEED?

FOOD AND WATER

- Diet will depend on the cat's age, lifestyle and state of health.
- Cats must have a well-balanced, meat-based diet. Cats cannot be vegetarians!
- How much a cat needs to eat depends on its diet, bodyweight and how active it is. However, they naturally eat several small meals a day.
- Cats need a constant supply of fresh, clean water.
- Always position your cat's feeding bowl well away from its litter tray (if you provide one).
- Adjust how much you feed your cat to make sure it doesn't become under or overweight.

A GOOD HOME

- Cats need a secure garden or safe area to play and exercise every day.
- You must provide somewhere comfortable, warm, dry and quiet where your cat can sleep undisturbed.
- They also need a safe place to hide if frightened — some cats feel safest when high up.
- Cats need easy access to go to the toilet. If your cat lives mostly indoors it can be trained to use a litter tray.
- If your cat doesn't go outdoors, make sure it has lots of toys and activities and enough space to exercise, climb and play.

COMPANY

- Cats that like other friendly cats and people should be able to mix with them for at least part of the day.
- Many cats are happier living without other cats. A cat may suffer if it can't avoid a cat it doesn't like.
- Unless introduced at an early age, cats will usually be scared of other animals, such as dogs.
- Cats that are treated kindly from an early age will see people as friends. But don't force a cat to mix with humans if it doesn't want to.
- Someone responsible must look after your cat when you're on holiday.

TO BEHAVE NORMALLY

- The way a cat behaves will depend on its age, personality and past experiences.
- Cats are naturally playful animals and many enjoy playing with toys and people.
- Cats sleep for many hours a day (sometimes up to 18!), but when awake they're active and need opportunities to exercise to stay fit and healthy.
- Provide your cat with a sturdy scratching post so that it can mark its territory and sharpen its claws. Make sure the post is tall enough for it to use fully stretched, especially if it doesn't go outside.
- Scratching is natural behaviour, so never punish your cat or shout at it for scratching, as it will become nervous and scared. Seek expert advice if your cat's behaviour becomes an ongoing problem.
- Cats that are ill, frightened or in pain may change their behaviour or develop unwanted habits. Watch out for any changes in your cat's behaviour. If you are in any doubt about your cat's health, contact your vet immediately.

TO BE HEALTHY

- Ask your vet for advice about things you can do to protect your cat's health, such as vaccination, neutering and treatment to control parasites, such as fleas and worms.
- Keep up to date with your cat's annual vaccinations.
- Neutering your cat will not only prevent unwanted litters, but will also reduce certain unwanted behaviour, such as spraying and roaming in male cats.
- Check your cat for injury or illness every day, and take it to a vet for a health check at least once a year. If you suspect your cat is poorly, ask an adult to take it to a vet immediately.
- Regular careful brushing (ask your vet to show you how to brush your cat the right way) is important to help keep your cat's coat in good condition and prevent hairballs. Regular grooming is especially important for long-haired cats.
- Help keep your cat's teeth healthy and keep up to date with regular veterinary dental checks.
- Make sure your cat can be identified by having it microchipped, so that it can be returned to you if it becomes lost.

YPA PHOTOGRAPHER AWARDS

Every year the RSPCA holds its own photography awards just for people like you! A vast array of animals have been snapped all over the world.

From guinea pigs in the garden to lions in Botswana – take a look here at some of the best entries we've had over the years. If you fancy taking part next year why not check out: www.rspca.org.uk/ypa? And remember, you don't need an expensive camera, just a love of animals!

Clockwise from top left
Orang-utan
Teah Higgs age 9
Overall winner 2006

Budgie in the sink
Helen Ford age 13
Overall winner 2004

Giraffe
Dominic Kent age 13
Runner-up 12-18 category 2004

Hippopotamus
Gareth Newton age 11
Overall winner 2003

RSPCA YOUNG PHOTOGRAPHER AWARDS

Clockwise from top left

Dog through fence
Daniel Beegan age 16
Commended 2007

Lion cubs
Matthew Burrard-Lucas age 17
Commended 12-18 category 2007

Calmer chameleon
Alex Worthington age 10
Overall winner 2007

Guinea pig
Caitlin Begley age 11
Commended pet personalities category 2007

Hard to swallow
Jodie Randall age 18
Runner-up 12-18 category 2007

Greek gratitude
Sarah Boulding age 13
Commended pet personalities category 2007

Tortoise
Lucy Todd age 18
Shortlisted finalist 2007

Clockwise from left

Insect
Charles Wright age 17
Winner The Olympus Portfolio category 2006

Frog
Sophie Livsey age 12
Winner under 12 years category 2007

African land snail
Bobbie Horseman age 11
Commended under 12 years category 2006

Guinea pig face
Emma Sture age 11
Runner-up under 12 years category 2003

Cat in flowerpot
Isabella Williams age 13
*Winner pet personalities
category 2007*

Puffin
Catriona Parfitt age 13
Runner-up 12-18 category 2006

Celebrity quotes!

We asked... and your fave celebs answered!

What's your favourite animal?

A kangaroo! They're great animals and are the symbol of Australia. Rolf Harris

Dogs, I love dogs. When I do eventually get one I would like a bulldog and I'd call it Spud. Gemma Atkinson

Probably cats, but I love all kinds of animals. Anna (*Toonattik*)

Tigers. I just wish I could give one a cuddle without it being scared and attacking me! Jamie (*Toonattik*)

I'm a big fan of sharks – people think I'm nuts! I've seen a lot of different sharks – whale sharks, great whites, bull sharks – and I always enjoy filming them, and it's usually quite an adrenaline rush! Michaela Strachan

I really like tortoises! Dani Harmer (*Tracy Beaker*)

A badger. Sam Nixon (*Sam and Mark*)

A giraffe. Mark Rhodes (*Sam and Mark*)

I love cats, but can't get too close because I'm allergic to them. Michelle (Liberty X)

I love monkeys! Jessica (Liberty X)

Tigers, because they are such beautiful animals. Kevin (Liberty X)

Jake's mate: Jake and his chocolate labrador, Dilys

Swimming with penguins was scary – they poo everywhere! Dom (Dick & Dom)

I love big cats. For my birthday my mum took me to a safari park. It was amazing... we met some tigers, which were extremely powerful, beautiful and very, very scary! Melanie C

Animals bring lots of comfort to so many people – they're our friends, our companions, our walking buddies, our babies, our source of cuddles. Anna (*Toonattik*)

What animal welfare issues concern you?

All of them! Fur and hens and whaling and animal testing and everything. I think it's all disgusting. Dakota Blue Richards (*The Golden Compass*)

The welfare of all animals is important to me. Cruelty to animals is so unnecessary, especially fur farming because all it comes down to is vanity

– there is no moral argument to support killing animals for their fur. Melanie C

Whaling. I hate the fact that not enough is being done about whalers. Jamie (*Toonattik*)

I think seal clubbing is morally wrong and completely unnecessary. Mark Rhodes

Are you afraid of any animals?

I don't like cockroaches.
Mark Rhodes

Any creepy-crawlies spook me!
Sam Nixon

I don't like alligators, crocodiles or poisonous snakes.
Rolf Harris

Working with lions for *On Safari*. There you are next to them trying to deliver your lines, then one roars and the noise is terrifying! Dick (Dick & Dom)

If you could be any animal, what would you be and why?

A scarlet macaw, but in the wild rather than caged, of course. I'd love to be able to fly, and just imagine being able to fly over the Amazon. Also, they are so smart and friendly – I spent several days watching them in Peru and they would hang out together, constantly calling to each other! They are just so full of character and stunning to look at too.
Charlotte Uhlenbroek

I would love to be a killer whale because essentially you're pretty much at the top of the food chain, so to roam the sea and be the king would be great!
JK (JK & Joel, *Hider in the House*)

I'd be one of the turtles in Finding Nemo. It would be great to cruise along in the lovely warm sea.
Jake Humphrey

An elephant once charged me when I surprised it, and I am quite lucky to still be here. *Charlotte Uhlenbroek*

Without a doubt I'd be a dolphin. Partly because I think it must be so fantastic to use the ocean as a playground, and they look like they're always smiling and I'm quite a smiley person. Plus, dolphins always work together and I really enjoy being part of a team.
Michaela Strachan

Seasonal tips

Winter

Summer

Brrr...illiant!

Keeping warm

When the cold weather comes and there isn't much food to live on, some animals decide the best option is simply to switch off and sleep until spring. Bats, hedgehogs and snakes are some of the many animals that go into this very deep sleep, called hibernation.

Before hibernating an animal eats more than usual so its body can live off its fat reserves while it sleeps. The animal then finds a safe spot to settle and, as it sleeps out the winter, its body temperature, heartbeat and breathing rate all lower to help it save energy.

Pond life

Many pond creatures go into a state of semi-hibernation. As most pond life is cold-blooded, they head to the bottom of the pond (where it's several degrees warmer) and hide out in a dormant state. One way to try and stop the pond from freezing over is to place a large ball (such as a football) on to the surface. The movement should stop the water underneath from freezing, so that when you take it away and swirl the water, valuable oxygen can get through to the creatures below.

Remember to replace the ball before ice starts to form over the hole, but if the water does freeze, don't break the ice as this can shock, and even kill, pond animals.

Garden wildlife

As food can be scarce in winter, some animals decide to store provisions during the summer months. Squirrels are very good at this and can be seen running up and down trees in the garden, picking and hiding nuts. Then, when there's no food available, they dig up the nuts that they buried earlier – and amazingly they know exactly where to find them!

The robin with its red breast is a welcome flash of colour in winter. It usually eats insects and worms, but during winter it can be hard to get worms out of the frozen ground. By putting out kitchen scraps – such as stale cake or bread (crumbled on to a bird table), cut-up bacon rind and crumbled or grated cheese – as well as fresh water, we can help these lovely birds through the winter. Remember, it's important to clean bird tables and any other bird feeders at least once a week with mild detergent.

Animals' needs change with the seasons. Wild animals need more food in winter and our pets need more water in the summer. Read on to discover how animals adapt to the ever-changing year and how you can help them survive...

The heat is on!

Netting nuisance

RSPCA inspectors are often called out to rescue wildlife caught in netting protecting ponds, fruit and vegetables. Snakes get tangled up most often, but other animals like hedgehogs, frogs and birds can also be caught. If these animals are not rescued they will not survive, so please make sure that netting is pulled tightly over crops and ponds. Tennis nets also need to be folded away when not in use.

Pond ramps

Hedgehogs often end up in ponds or swimming pools – most fall in accidentally while taking a drink. Although hedgehogs can swim, they need an escape route or they could drown. So it's a good idea to place a ramp or a wire 'scrambling' net in the pond to help them crawl back on to dry land.

Mower mayhem

Strimmers and lawnmowers can be deadly to wildlife so look out for slow-moving animals. Hedgehogs curl up if they are scared and frogs and toads crouch down rather than run away.

Water worry

If you have a bird bath please make sure it's cleaned at least every week with a mild detergent, rinsed thoroughly and topped up with fresh water every day. Then sit back and watch our feathered friends enjoying a bath!

Your pet needs plenty of water. If it gets too hot it may not be able to cool down quickly enough. The golden rule is to never leave an animal where the temperature could become very high, such as in a conservatory or car, where it can reach more than 50°C (120°F) – which is extremely hot – because if it can't escape the heat it could die.

Remember too that the sun's rays move – although your pet may start out in the shade, it could soon be in direct sunlight. Even in the shade temperatures can become dangerously hot.

If you think your pet is suffering from heat stroke, soak it with cool (not cold) water and take it to the vet immediately. Ensure that you don't soak your pet so much that it begins to shiver. A word of caution – if a dog is suffering from heat stroke, it will probably be very anxious and start to panic. So watch out because it may bite.

Sunblock

Please remember to put sunblock on light-coloured pets. This can be non-toxic, waterproof, human sunblock (a children's or baby's sunblock is best) or one made specifically for pets. Sunburn can cause skin cancer in animals as well as humans, so beware. There's no need to put sunblock all over your pet – just on the white tips of an animal's ears that are exposed to the sun's rays.

Ask the vets!

We receive lots of letters from Animal Action readers concerned about their pet's health or behaviour. We asked two of our very own vets about some of your most common questions. So read on as Wendy Stickells from Putney Animal Hospital and Rachel Kirkby from the Greater Manchester Animal Hospital help you with your pet-care concerns...

RACHEL

WENDY

Why does my cat sometimes eat grass?

WENDY SAYS: Some cats love to eat grass. No one knows the reason why, but there are a few theories.

Eating grass can help your cat to bring up fur balls, which can build up in their stomach as they groom. Grass is also thought to help their digestion, although cats don't need it as part of their diet as they are carnivores, which means they only eat meat.

If cats feel nauseous, or have an inflamed stomach, they may eat grass to help themselves be sick as this relieves the nausea or stomach ache. If your cat eats grass and is often sick then it would be worth a visit to your vet to rule out any stomach problems.

Cats can also eat grass because it is fun, so let them play!

My poor dog hates travelling in the car and is sick every time. What can I do to help?

WENDY SAYS: Dogs are often car sick because they think travelling in the car could be a scary or unpleasant experience. So the best way to help your dog is to make the journey less stressful for

your dog — you could start by trying to make the car a safe, 'happy' place.

Sit in the car with your dog with the engine off so that he or she can get used to being inside it. Give treats so your dog starts to associate the car with a reward. Once you have done this a few times, try letting the engine run but without the car moving — and gradually increase the time spent with your dog in the stationary car. Once your dog is ready, try him or her with a five-minute car journey and then go for a nice walk afterwards. Increase the journey time a little at a time and always offer a reward when the journey is over.

Open windows can also help distract your dog while on the journey, just make sure he or she is secure. If none of this helps, contact your vet.

My rabbit has white flecks in her fur that look like dandruff. What shall I do?

WENDY SAYS: When a rabbit has dandruff, it often means that your rabbit has mites that live on the skin, which are called *cheyletiella*. They will make your rabbit itch and sometimes the mites can live on human skin and may make you itch as well! Take your rabbit to the vet to get medication to kill the mites and get rid of the dandruff. And if you have a problem with your skin itching, then visit your doctor!

I've noticed that my cat has a really rough tongue! Why is this?

RACHEL SAYS: Cats' tongues are rough for two reasons. The roughness helps them groom themselves and keep their coats beautiful and matt-free. It also helps cats hold onto food and their prey.

My dog's breath smells! Is there anything I can do?

RACHEL SAYS: A dog's breath will often smell when there is a build up of tartar on its teeth — just like your breath would if you never cleaned your teeth! I would take your dog along to your local vet and get its teeth checked out. The vet may suggest that your dog needs its teeth cleaning. Once the vet has removed all the plaque you could then brush your dog's teeth every day with a special dog toothpaste and a soft toothbrush.

My two guinea pigs often eat their own poo! Is this bad for them?

RACHEL SAYS: Guinea pigs produce two different types of droppings. The first type is soft and moist and your guinea pig will eat these as soon they are produced – it does this to make sure it gets as many nutrients as possible from its food. The second type of droppings are hard and black and your guinea pig won't eat these.

Sometimes my goldfish come to the top of the tank and float on their sides. Are they unwell?

RACHEL SAYS: It sounds like your fish are suffering from swim bladder disease. The swim bladder is a little air sac inside the goldfish that helps it float or sink in the water. When your fish are floating on their sides it means they have too much air in their swim bladder. This, like most fish diseases, is usually due to poor water quality. You need to do a partial water change and check that your filter is working well.

My pet rats chew the bars of their cage. Why do they do this and could it hurt them?

WENDY SAYS: Rats are very intelligent animals that just love mental stimulation. Sometimes they chew the bars of their cages because they are bored, so make sure you provide them with lots of toys and spend time playing with them – this can be very rewarding for you and your pets!

It may be worth a trip to your vet to check that your rats' teeth are not overgrown as they can sometimes chew the bars to try to keep their teeth short and sharp. Wooden chews for your rats to gnaw on are available from pet shops and these should help prevent their teeth from overgrowing.

You could also put a mineral block – again, available from pet shops – in their cage, as occasionally rats can chew their bars if they are lacking in certain minerals.

Why is it so important to have my puppy spayed?

WENDY SAYS: Spaying is a procedure where an animal's ovaries and uterus are removed and there are a number of reasons why this is a good idea for your puppy. Firstly, if you have your puppy spayed this will reduce the risk, or prevent, a number of very serious health problems such as mammary (breast) cancer, ovarian cancer, womb cancer and a life-threatening illness called pyometra, which would mean that your dog would need to have an emergency spay operation that is quite risky. When a puppy is spayed, it prevents her from coming into heat twice a year meaning that she's not at risk of getting pregnant. RSPCA rescue centres are full of dogs that need homes, so if your dog has pups even more dogs will need to be rehomed. All the dog-owning vets I know have their dogs neutered at the first opportunity to prevent these problems – seems it's the right thing to do for your puppy.

My cat wees indoors! Why does he do this and is there anything I can do to stop it?

WENDY SAYS: There can be lots of reasons for this including cystitis, bladder crystals, diabetes, kidney disease and urinary tract problems. These can cause a cat to wee inappropriately, so it's worth taking your pet to your vet for a thorough exam to rule out these problems.

If there's no sign of disease causing him to wee in the house then it is more likely to be behavioural. For example, cats hate using a dirty litter tray, and if it's not cleaned at least once a day, your cat may feel he can't reuse it and go elsewhere in the house instead. Also if you have more than one cat, then more than one tray in the house can help. Does your cat have access to outdoors, and if so, do any neighbourhood cats come in the house and upset him? If so, he may be marking his territory – maybe consider getting a magnetic cat flap.

When you clean up his wee, he may think another cat has had a wee there and he'll need to mark the spot again – using biological washing liquid then surgical spirit can get rid of the smell rather than normal household cleaning products.

Stress, which can be caused by a new pet or person in the house, can bring on weeing. Your vet can tell you about pheromone diffusers/sprays that release smells which may relax your cat a little and there are also new drugs available that may help.

My dog is very vocal and sometimes barks and barks for no reason! It can be embarrassing and very disturbing. Why does he do this?

WENDY SAYS: Dogs are naturally pack animals and barking is a normal part of dogs' behaviour – however, it can be very loud and hard to deal with! If your dog barks when you leave him alone it could be related to him being very distressed as he is lonely and seeking attention. Dogs also bark as a way of defending their territory, for example when someone comes into your house. If your dog barks any other time I would advise taking him to see an animal behaviourist who can assess what is making him bark and will suggest ways of reducing it to make everyone's lives more peaceful and happy!

Pet Care

Visit your local library or use the internet to find out more information on your specific pet.

THE RIGHT PET FOR YOU?

Rabbits are difficult to look after. They need lots of space, careful handling and other friendly rabbits to live with. They also need large homes that can be expensive to create. Rabbits live for five to 10 years so the decision to buy a rabbit should not be taken lightly.

Rabbits

WHAT DO RABBITS NEED?

FOOD AND WATER

- A rabbit's diet is 80-90 per cent hay, but they also enjoy grass and small amounts of high-fibre rabbit pellets. Apples, carrots, dandelions and other vegetables can be given in small quantities.
- Adjust how much you feed your rabbit to make sure it doesn't become under or overweight.
- A constant supply of fresh, clean drinking water in a drip feed bottle with metal spout should be provided.
- Rabbits eat some of their own droppings! This is called coprophagy and is perfectly normal behaviour, essential for their health.

A GOOD HOME

- Rabbits must have a large living enclosure with a quiet, cosy shelter for sleeping, a toilet area, a feeding area and lots and lots of space to exercise.
- Rabbits prefer to use separate areas for sleeping, feeding and going to the toilet, so their enclosure should let them do this.
- Rabbits need places to hide if they feel frightened. These 'refuges' should have at least two exits to prevent dominant rabbits becoming aggressive to other rabbits inside them. There should be as many refuges as there are rabbits, plus one more. Cardboard boxes with cut-out exits make good refuges.
- Rabbits urinate heavily so it's a good idea to provide them with a litter tray filled with newspaper and hay. This will help when you clean it out every day.
- Provide your rabbits with appropriate bedding to keep them clean and comfortable.
- Any home must be safe from predators.

- Rabbits chew lots, so you may need to 'rabbit-proof' your home if your rabbits are house rabbits or are sometimes brought indoors. Electric cables will need to be covered, any houseplants should not be toxic to rabbits, and your rabbits should be prevented from going into potentially dangerous areas of the house.

COMPANY

- Rabbits are very sociable and should live with other friendly rabbits, unless there is a good welfare reason not to. A rabbit made to live alone may suffer.
- You should not keep male and female rabbits together once they are sexually mature (at around four months old) unless you have them neutered.
- Rabbits should be provided with refuges/shelters so that they can avoid mixing/contact with other rabbits if they want to.
- The widespread practice of keeping rabbits and guinea pigs together is not recommended because they have different diets, they can fight, and can spread diseases to one another.
- Rabbits must be looked after by a responsible person when you are on holiday.

TO BEHAVE NORMALLY

- Rabbits are active, athletic animals and need plenty of space. They must have daily freedom to hop around in a large, safe area and preferably to graze.
- Rabbits are easily frightened and must have places to hide.
- Rabbits are curious animals that like to play, so it's a good idea to give them lots of suitable, safe toys to keep them amused. Hay bales to jump on, untreated apple wood to gnaw and cardboard boxes make fun cheap toys for rabbits.
- Rabbits burrow so make sure that you safeguard any enclosure.

TO BE HEALTHY

- Check your rabbit for injury or illness every day, and take it to a vet for a health check at least once a year. If you suspect your rabbit is poorly, ask an adult to take it to a vet immediately.
- Ask your vet for advice on how you can protect your rabbit's health, such as vaccination, neutering and treatments to control parasites (e.g. fleas and worms).
  - A rabbit's teeth never stop growing, but as long as the animal is being provided with the correct diet (hay-based), this shouldn't be a problem. Contact your vet if you are at all concerned about your rabbit's teeth and have regular dental checks.
- Carefully groom your rabbit regularly (ask your vet to show you how to brush your rabbit the right way), especially if it is a long-haired breed.

Real-life RESCUES

Kitten-kaboodle!

Four kittens abandoned in a Nottinghamshire lay-by have been rehomed. The two boys, Tim and Tom, went to one new owner and Jade and Jordan (now renamed Tom and Jerry!), the two tiny tortoiseshell girls, went to another.

Michelle Booth and her two daughters, Jessica and Megan, lost their 12-year-old cat Elsa in summer 2007, but really wanted another cat and had thought about rehoming an adult. But when they met Tom and Jerry, everything changed…

The family went along to the RSPCA Radcliffe-on-Trent Animal Centre in Nottinghamshire to see if any cats were looking for a new home. There they met these adorable balls of fluff – kittens that had had a scary start in life and were looking for a second chance.

The Booths love their kittens, spending hours playing with them and making them feel safe.

Oliver's tale

Would you believe that this lovely spaniel-cross was once a mange-ridden puppy, dumped in woods in Lincoln by his cruel owner?

An RSPCA animal collection officer picked Oliver up and took him to a vet. Mange is a horrible infection that affects an animal's skin, making it very itchy and sore.

But Oliver responded well to treatment and was soon ready to go to a foster family to be looked after. He couldn't stay at an animal centre as mange is highly contagious, but he could stay at a wildlife centre in isolation – as these places take in mangy foxes all the time!

The parents of one of the centre's staff members couldn't resist Oliver and decided to give him a permanent home, and now he's grown up into a gorgeous dog!

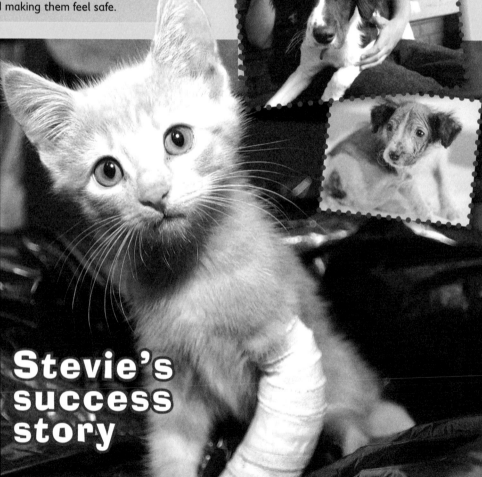

A kitten with a broken leg, abandoned with its mother in a bin liner, has been rescued and rehomed by the RSPCA.

Stevie, believed to be about eight weeks old, was discovered by a passer-by who saw a bag moving in a gutter in a suburb of Bolton, near Manchester. When she looked inside she found the terrified kitten and his mother.

Cathy Kay from the RSPCA Bolton Branch collected the pair and took them for veterinary treatment. And although Stevie was very active, it was obvious his leg was broken.

The vet put a splint on the kitten's leg and bandaged it to help it mend. Cathy said: "Stevie was growing so fast that we had to take him to the vet every three or four days to have the bandage re-set."

Cathy and her colleagues placed a story in the local newspaper and after dozens of offers to rehome him, Stevie went to live in Southport. His mother was also successfully rehomed.

Stevie's success story

A new life for Geri

A starving dog found dumped in a box in West Sussex has made a full recovery and settled in to her new home. Geri went from weighing just four kilos to more than 17 before she was rehomed with a family in Crawley.

The small, tan cross-bred bitch was found by a police officer in a cardboard box in a lay-by. She was collected and quickly taken to a vet by an RSPCA inspector who said she was the thinnest dog she had ever seen.

Geri steadily gained weight and was eventually taken to the RSPCA Mount Noddy Animal Home near Chichester, where Chris Hathaway, his partner Debbie and their children fell in love with her.

The family discussed rehoming Geri for a week before returning to Mount Noddy. A few days later Geri was in her new home, starting her new life with a new name – Missy.

Lucky Lola

When this foal was two weeks old and just three-quarters of a metre high she was abandoned in a Nottinghamshire field. It is thought the foal was left by someone driving past the field early in the morning.

The foal was spotted trying to suckle milk from a pony. The pony's owner contacted the RSPCA and an inspector took the foal to a local equine rescue home where she was given a comfy straw bed and lots of much-needed milk.

The poor foal was suffering from diarrhoea but was otherwise bright and lively. Staff at the rescue centre called her Lola and hand-reared her. She stayed at the rescue centre until she was healthy enough to be rehomed.

Terrific trio!

These three kittens, who fought for their lives in a bin that was quickly filling with rainwater, were rehomed and are all now having the time of their lives!

All three kittens were successfully rehomed by staff at the RSPCA's Gonsal Farm Animal Centre in Shrewsbury – Lily went first, leaving George and Daisy to be offered a home. Thankfully, when Charlotte Vaughan, from Stafford, saw the pair on the centre's website, she knew she had to go and see them.

Staff were keen for them to be rehomed together so Charlotte, who grew up with cats, agreed to take them both. "George gets into everything, he's so mischievous," said Charlotte. "He's even been up the chimney! It's hard to believe they were so timid when I first got them – now they're completely changed kittens, really playful. And they both have a thing about loo roll! If I leave the bathroom door open, they help themselves to the toilet paper and shred it!"

Charlotte added: "Out of all the cats I've had in my life, I have never had so much appreciation, love and affection as I have from George and Daisy. They seem so grateful. I'm so happy it was me who adopted them."

T-shirts to

As soon as your friends see you wearing your funky tie-dyed T-shirt, they are bound to want one too!

Cover your work area with large plastic bags or newspaper. And keep a supply of paper towels handy!

dye for!

1 Wash the T-shirt and work with it damp. Pinch the centre into a cone shape. Now wind an elastic band tightly around the top of the cone. Add more rubber bands at intervals until you reach the end of the cone.

2 Fill the container with enough cold water to cover the T-shirt. Follow the mixing instructions on the dye and add to the container. Dissolve the salt and cold fix in hot water and add to the container.

3 Put the T-shirt into the container and stir around with a wooden spoon. Keep stirring for about 10 minutes to make sure that the dye gets into the folds. Then stir every now and then for the next 50 minutes.

4 Lift the T-shirt out of the dye mix and rinse it really well in cold water. Take the elastic bands off and wash the T-shirt in soapy water. Hang it up to dry and in no time at all it will be ready to wear!

Pet Care

THE RIGHT PET FOR YOU?

Owning a horse or pony is extremely rewarding, but very hard work. You need a lot of land, time, money, commitment and experience. These animals will usually live for more than 20 years, so owning a horse or pony is a huge commitment.

RSPCA

ANIMAL Action

WOMBAT

Fly Aw

Make this jolly, fluttery mobile and hang it in your bedroom. Your friends will be really impressed and will probably want one too!

WHAT YOU NEED

- Pencil
- Coloured card
- Ruler
- Scissors
- Coloured paper
- Cord
- Sparkly 'jewels'
- Glue
- 2 x 35cm lengths of dowel (wood)

1 Draw a bird shape, like the ones here, on a piece of coloured card. It should measure about 15cm from tip of tail to beak. Cut it out and use as a pattern to trace around four more times on coloured card. Cut out the shapes and cut 2cm slits to slot the wings through.

2 Cut five rectangles of coloured paper 20cm x 16cm. Starting from one of the shorter ends, fold the rectangle backwards and forwards to make concertina folds. Keep the folds together and poke the wings through the slits in the birds.

3 Cut five lengths of thin cord to attach the birds to the dowel. Fan the wings out and glue the ends together, sandwiching a length of cord between them. Glue sparkly 'jewels' on either side of the birds' heads for eyes.

4 Put one of the lengths of dowel on top of the other to make a cross. Wind a length of string round and round the join and finish with a knot. Tie a length of cord to the join to hang the mobile up with. Finally, knot the birds in position!

Take a walk on the Wild Side

A day in the life of veterinary officer David Couper, based at RSPCA West Hatch Wildlife Centre in Somerset.

8.30am The day begins with the admission of a young barn owl, found by the side of the road.

It has a fractured wing and was probably hit by a car. A lot of young animals are admitted at this time of year, having been hit by cars as they look for territories of their own.

I examine the owl and fortunately, apart from its damaged wing and being slightly dehydrated, it seems fine. I give it fluids and it is anaesthetised and X-rayed. Both the radius and ulna (the two bones in the lower wing) are broken so the owl is prepared for surgery. I place a metal pin in the ulna, which I will leave in for about three weeks while the fractures heal, and the bird is put on a course of antibiotics.

10am My next patient is a mute swan with lead poisoning. The swan arrived two weeks ago in a very weak state – it couldn't even walk without help or lift its neck. Lead poisoning is fairly common in swans that have swallowed abandoned fishing weights.

After intravenous fluids and treatment for the lead poisoning the swan has gradually improved. Today it's standing and is a lot brighter. I take another blood sample to check that its blood lead levels are now OK.

1pm Animal collection officer Steve Powell brings in a weak and very thin grey seal pup found on a beach in Cornwall. It's only three or four weeks old so would have been recently weaned off its mother's milk. It's probably been struggling to find food in the recent stormy weather. I examine the seal – it has laboured breathing, discharge from both nostrils, and a few scratches from the rocks.

I take a blood sample to look for evidence of infection and start the seal on a course of antibiotics in case of pneumonia. Today it will be tube-fed a rehydrating, vitamin-rich fluid before progressing to a 'fish soup' (a special fish mixture) and eventually whole fish over the coming weeks. When it's feeding for itself we'll send it to the National Seal Sanctuary in Gweek, Cornwall, to mix with other seals before being returned to the wild.

3pm Elsewhere in the hospital it's time to open the hatches on some of our release aviaries, where a number of the birds reared by staff over the spring and summer, have been kept. Once the hatches are open, food will still be provided in the aviaries and the birds will be able to come and go as they please until they can fend for themselves.

5pm I take the advantage of a quiet moment to catch up with some paperwork. You never know what's going to arrive next at West Hatch!

A day in the life of RSPCA veterinary surgeon Steve Bexton, based at East Winch Wildlife Centre in Norfolk.

9.30am An RSPCA ambulance arrives with the day's first wildlife casualty – a mute swan with fishing line hanging from its beak. It is booked in at the reception desk with details of exactly where it was found so that it can be returned to its home area once recovered.

One of the wildlife assistants examines the swan to determine its level of shock and stress before giving it time to settle after the ambulance journey.

I begin my ward round, checking up on the hospital's in-patients. Winter is a quieter time than summer, but we still have nearly 200 wildlife patients at the hospital.

10am I check over one of our longer-term patients, a common seal pup called Comma. She was found on a nearby beach with breathing difficulties and a nasty cough caused by lungworms. Her course of treatment has finished and she is much better now so I give the go-ahead for her to be moved to a larger pool where she will have to compete with other seals for fish. This will help make her fit enough for release back into the wild.

11.45am I re-check the swan admitted earlier. X-rays reveal it has swallowed a fishing hook that's become lodged in its throat. We anaesthetise the bird and manage to carefully remove the hook using an endoscope (a tube with a tiny camera on the end). This means we won't have to operate and the swan will recover quickly and be able to go home earlier.

2pm After lunch I check on a young roe deer that was brought to us three days ago after being hit by a car. Although it wasn't seriously injured, the deer has been acting as though it is blind since it came in. This often happens to deer that are involved in road accidents, especially if they are hit on the head. The temporary blindness actually calms the deer, helping them cope with the stressful experience. Fortunately, most

deer completely regain their sight after a week or two. At this time of year we see a lot of wildlife casualties that have been hit by vehicles on dark evenings, so please keep a look out for animals on the roads at night.

3.45pm Among our latest arrivals is a hedgehog that needs immediate treatment. Unfortunately he'd fallen asleep in a garden bonfire pile, which had then been lit. The gardener spotted him just in time, pulled him out of the fire and rushed him to the centre. Luckily, the hedgehog only has a few burnt spines and some smoke inhalation. I've put him on a course of antibiotics and painkillers and moved him to our small-animal ward where the wildlife assistants will keep an eye on him.

6pm Before I leave I re-check the swan that arrived this morning. He's made a full recovery from the procedure and should be ready to return to the wild in a day or two.

Pet Care

THE RIGHT PET FOR YOU?

Budgies and canaries are colourful and friendly companions that need to live with other birds in a large aviary. This can be expensive to build or buy and needs regular cleaning to keep your birds healthy. Budgies can live for up to 10 years, canaries for five to six.

For the first time in its 184-year history the RSPCA is running a donkey centre. Lockwood Donkey Centre in Surrey was left to the RSPCA when its owner died, so the Society took up the reins and is now the guardian of 25 donkeys, several horses and ponies, two llamas, an unusual pig, two sheep, and various cats and dogs! Why not take a look around?

MEET THE GANG!

Here are just a few of the Lockwood donkeys. They range from eight years to more than 30 years old – donkeys can live a long time! All have names, and their own personalities. Most have ended up at Lockwood because they were unwanted pets, elderly or sick. Some people buy donkeys without realising the hard work involved in keeping them, or how long they live.

Kay Lockwood, who owned the centre until she died, was a well-known and respected woman who loved donkeys and wanted to help them. With her husband John, she started the centre about 40 years ago. When the number of donkeys began to grow Mrs Lockwood took on some staff to help with the day-to-day duties such as cleaning out and feeding the animals. Today, there are eight members of staff and they all adore the animals there.

HANDSOME JAKE

Meet Jake. What a handsome chap! Jake has perfect manners and gets on well with the other Lockwood donkeys and the staff. Jake and most of his stable mates can be adopted, which means you pay Lockwood Donkey Centre an amount of money for a year and are then kept up to date with 'your' donkey's life at Lockwood. You can check out: www.lockwooddonkeycentre.org.uk for more information.

So far, the RSPCA has spent £120,000 on important repairs to the stables, outbuildings and grounds to make sure that donkeys like Jake are safe and well looked after. Lots more money needs to be spent on the centre, so staff will be thinking of cool fundraising ideas for you to be involved with!

STABLE MATES

Here are Janice and Lester. Janice is available for adoption but Lester isn't – he's one of the older donkeys and is probably more than 30 years old. Janice is quite a beauty – maybe that's why all the boy donkeys try to flirt with her!

Lester is soooo handsome – his coat has a beautiful tint of red in the summer and he has the softest nose ever! He's very intelligent and craves love and affection, which Sophie, one of the centre's supervisors, is very happy to give him. He has a long coat so has to be groomed more often than the other donkeys. He makes Sophie laugh because when she's finished grooming him, Lester will follow her around and nudge her as if to say: "Groom me again, please!"

Dreaming of donkeys

CHEEKY CHAPPIE!

What do you think of gorgeous miniature Shetland pony Silver? Isn't he handsome? Staff at Lockwood Donkey Centre couldn't resist 15-year-old Silver and his friends – 12-year-old Bert, and nine-year-olds Gavin and Peter – when their previous owner had to give them up suddenly. They will be brilliantly looked after at Lockwood until a permanent home can be found for them.

Unlike ponies, miniature Shetlands aren't measured in "hands" because they're too small – they're just measured in centimetres instead. Silver stands a full 87.5cm tall.

MAJOR MISCHIEF!

Eeyore! Look at these two – it's Dolly and Jake. Dolly is seen here with Jake but she's usually with Nicholas, her true partner! Dolly is a carefree donkey who loves ginger biscuits, and is one of the donkeys in the adoption scheme.

Jonathan Silk, the RSPCA's regional manager and the person who is in overall charge of Lockwood Donkey Centre, said: "What is it about donkeys? I know they have their moments, but on the whole they seem such contented, trusting creatures. When I watch them, it seems to me that, as long as they are looked after well, they're just happy with their existence; they ask for no more."

The miniature Shetlands, as well as most of the donkeys at Lockwood, can be adopted. For more information click on: **www.lockwooddonkeycentre.org.uk;** write to: Freepost RRXB-XSSE-TZSB, Lockwood Donkey Centre, Pinner HA5 1TW; call 01428 687 749; or e-mail: enquiries@lockwooddonkeycentre.org.uk.

Pet care

THE RIGHT PET FOR YOU?

Tortoises and terrapins are specialist pets that require specific care. Temperature, humidity and light levels are factors to get absolutely right if you decide that a tortoise or terrapin is the right pet for you. Be aware though - tortoises can live for more than 50 years, and terrapins for 30, so these creatures need long-term commitment.

Tortoises and terrapins

FOOD AND WATER

- Your tortoise must have access to a shallow bowl of fresh, clean water.
- Most tortoises are herbivores and eat grass, clover, dandelions, greens, leafy weeds and sometimes tomatoes. Terrapins are omnivores and eat anything from fish and freshwater shrimp to earthworms and cheese!

A GOOD HOME

- Pet terrapins live in a large glass tank (about one square metre per terrapin). Make sure your terrapin has access to dry land for resting, basking and walking around, and an area of fresh water for swimming and eating.
- A tortoise needs a large enclosure where it can roam about, containing within it a nesting or sleeping area with suitable nesting material.
- Ask your local tortoise/terrapin specialist about suitable heat sources and lighting so that your terrapin or tortoise can correctly warm up or cool down, and stay at the correct humidity level.

COMPANY

- Some tortoises prefer to live alone and other species prefer company. Research the type of tortoise or terrapin you're thinking about getting and you will know how many you can keep together.
- Most terrapins can be grouped together as long as all are of a similar size.

TO BEHAVE NORMALLY

- Most tortoises naturally like to burrow, hide and bathe in shallow water, so make sure you provide an environment that allows for this.
- Terrapins like to swim and spend time on land so it is important to provide an environment that allows for this.

- If your tortoise hibernates, make sure it is well fed and healthy to see it through hibernation. Terrapins kept in vivariums don't hibernate.

TO BE HEALTHY

- Check your tortoise or terrapin every day for signs of illness or injury and take it to a specialist vet if unwell or injured.
- Don't oil or scratch your tortoise's shell because it can block the pores, attract dirt and increase the risk of infection.
- Annual vet checks should help prevent disease, but seek advice from a specialist vet if you are concerned about the health of your tortoise or terrapin.
- Terrapins often carry salmonella, so wash your hands thoroughly after cleaning their terrarium or touching them.
- Make sure you have a responsible person to look after your pet when you go on holiday.

Seahorse

FACT FILE

● Seahorses belong to a group of animals known as Hippocampus; this name comes from the Greek word for horse (hippos) and sea monster (campus).

● Seahorses are thought to have been around for 40 million years.

● They don't swim very fast so they have to rely on being camouflaged to avoid being eaten. They are masters of disguise and gradually change colour to disappear into their surroundings, and sometimes grow fine filaments over their body to mimic seaweed.

● They use their long snouts for sucking up and eating their food and will eat living prey, including small crustaceans such as shrimp. In fact they are able to consume up to 3,000 brine shrimp a day!

● Seahorses can live up to five years in the wild but sadly many are caught and killed for medicinal purposes or kept alive for aquariums.

● Can you believe that the male seahorse gives birth to the offspring? The female deposits her eggs into the male's pouch where he fertilises them and gives birth to hundreds of babies a couple of weeks later.

RSPCA

ANIMAL
Action

GREY SEAL

Animal myths

Over the years people have had some pretty funny ideas about animals – things that we now know are completely untrue! But how did these beastly blunders come about, and what's the truth behind each odd tale?

EVER HEARD THE SAYING 'AS BLIND AS A BAT'?

As bats are nocturnal (active at night) many people presume that as they don't need their eyesight it doesn't work. In fact, around sunset, most bats can probably see better than humans. Then, after dark, when eyesight would be largely redundant, they use something called 'echolocation', which works by sending out sounds which bounce back to them like an echo. This directs them as they fly up to 30mph through the night skies, catching thousands of insects along the way!

OSTRICHES
BURY THEIR HEADS IN THE SAND

If you're trying to ignore a problem someone might say you are 'burying your head in the sand', and it was once thought that this is what ostriches did. Well, as these large birds don't actually live in the desert, they don't really have sand to bury their head in! But they do rest their heads on the ground when they are under threat. This natural instinct is designed to make predators believe that the ostrich's body is just a small bush!

SNAKES
HYPNOTISE THEIR PREY BEFORE ATTACKING

It certainly looks like they do because, as snakes have no moveable eyelids, their eyes are always open – even when they're sleeping. So, they don't actually hypnotise their prey but their wide, staring eyes make it look as though they are!

IF YOU HANDLE A TOAD IT WILL GIVE YOU WARTS

Well, if you lived hundreds of years ago you might have thought this to be true. Warts are caused by a virus that can be spread through contact, so the toad, which has wart-like bumps on its body, was thought to be highly contagious. In fact, a toad's bumps are not warts at all but glands which contain a toxic substance designed to keep predators away.

ELEPHANTS ARE AFRAID OF MICE

Elephants are very sensitive creatures and are wary of sudden sounds and movements. Back in Roman times, when they were used as transport – particularly during wars – pigs were often thrust into the poor elephants' faces by the enemy, which would frighten them away. It was probably the squeal of the pig, rather than the pig itself, which caused this reaction. And over the years, elephants became known for being scared of any high-pitched sounds, including the squeak of a mouse!

THE GIRAFFE IS THE OFFSPRING OF THE CAMEL AND THE LEOPARD

This idea might make you giggle, but it's completely untrue! When early Europeans first saw this amazing creature they assumed it must be a hybrid – a mixture – of two different animals. They thought the giraffe had the long neck and manner of walking of a camel but the spots of a leopard. In fact, the giraffe is more closely related to deer and cattle than any other animal.

HEDGEHOGS STEAL APPLES BY ROLLING THEIR SPIKES OVER THEM AND CARRYING THEM ON THEIR BACK

Wouldn't that be a funny sight! But unfortunately you're not likely to ever see a hedgehog carrying an apple on its back – so why would anyone ever think this? Well, fallen apples are often found with tiny little holes in them, and sometimes there are hedgehogs munching away nearby – but these days we know that the tiny holes are likely to have been caused by insects, not the hedgehogs' spikes!

Pet Care

Visit your local library or use the internet to find out more information on your specific pet.

THE RIGHT PET FOR YOU?

If you're interested in keeping parrots, the RSPCA recommends that you research the care of these creatures very carefully before buying one. Parrots are colourful, intelligent and can make good pets, but need a lot of space, time and commitment. They can live for 50 years or more!

Parrots

WHAT DO PARROTS NEED?

🐾 FOOD AND WATER

- Most of the parrots' diets are based around a range of seeds and nuts, although some prefer nectar. Most species will require fruit – such as apples, pears and bananas – and vegetables – such as broccoli, sugar snap peas and carrots. But most important for good health is a full, varied diet providing balanced nutrition.
- Make sure your parrot has access to fresh, clean water. A small bowl or tower-type water container can be clipped onto the side of the cage.

🏠 A GOOD HOME

- A parrot needs more space than it is usually given. Most cages do not allow most parrots any space to fly, but provision should be made for all parrots to be able to fly between a variety of perches.
- Perches should be made of natural material, of varying dimensions and placed at varying heights in an aviary – this will give the parrot interest and exercise.
- Some species are well adapted to the British climate and can be kept outdoors all year in a sheltered aviary. Others will require indoor accommodation and extra heating during many of the colder months.

💛 COMPANY

- Almost all parrot species prefer company of their own kind. However, given suitable alternative company, some species may be kept singly.

🐾 TO BEHAVE NORMALLY

- Parrots like to fly and climb so they must be provided with space and materials. Twigs and branches of fruit trees (e.g. apple, pear, cherry) make good climbing frames and also provide something to chew on.
  - As they are intelligent animals, other 'toys' will interest them, such as bells, chains and sets of keys, as well as whole fruits and seed heads such as millet sprays.
  - Parrots should be allowed to fly in an aviary or other secure area.

✚ TO BE HEALTHY

- Make sure you can spot the signs of illness in your parrot so you can take it to a vet for a check-up.
- Take advice on how the bird's diet and behaviour will change as it gets older so that you know how best to interact with it and provide the right care, environment and companionship.
- Good hygiene is very important, so you should make sure to wash and rinse your bird's water containers regularly.
- Check that the person who looks after your parrot when you go on holiday knows all about the care needed, including the specialist feeding and how to minimise any disturbance.

Don't forget that there are many local bird societies and interest groups that can advise you on your parrot.

Take a walk on the wild side

Two days in the life of wildlife supervisor Andrew Smith, based at RSPCA Stapeley Grange Wildlife Centre in Cheshire.

DAY ONE

8am This morning I'm working in the isolation unit, where larger animals like foxes, badgers and swans are housed when first admitted and may stay if they need treatment. One of the first patients is a poorly male swan (or cob) that's been shot in the neck with an airgun. I clean the cubicle, give the swan some fresh food and make him comfortable.

9.30am In one of the cubicles is a badger that was admitted to the centre a week ago after being hit by a car. Road traffic accidents are one of the main reasons badgers are admitted to the Society's wildlife centres. This badger has responded well to treatment and is ready to be let in to one of the outside isolation runs before he's released back to the wild in a few days. We try to return adult badgers to where they were found, as they are part of a social group with an established territory.

11.15am The vet checks the shot swan and decides to put him to sleep to prevent further suffering. This case is particularly sad as we know his mate is in the middle of building a nest ready for laying eggs.

12.30pm My next job is to check on a barn owl that's also been hit by a car. Barn owls swoop quite low across roads so it's not unusual for cars to hit them. Fortunately, this one looks like it will make a full recovery.

I clean the owl's cage, but don't feed it because the nocturnal animals are fed at night, as they would not eat during the day in the wild.

3.30pm Probably the most rewarding part of my job is returning rehabilitated wild animals to the wild, and today we are releasing two young collared doves that came in to the centre as orphans one month ago. Pigeons and doves breed all year round if the weather is suitable and this year they seem to have bred right through the mild winter. In fact, we admitted the first juvenile collared dove on 2 January!

The birds are taken to a local garden in an area where there's plenty of food available on people's bird tables. Once in the garden, I carefully open the box and the doves fly to the safety of the surrounding trees. We have ringed them so if these birds come to the centre again, we will know we've met them before!

5pm My last job today is preparing the food for seven hedgehogs that are in one of our outside enclosures. Like the barn owl, hedgehogs are nocturnal so they are fed at night with a mixture of dog food and a special dried food.

Any hedgehogs that visit your garden will love this concoction too!

DAY TWO

8am I begin work in one of the 'small bird' rooms, where we house injured pigeons, doves and garden birds. It's quiet in here at the moment, but in fledgling season it will be very noisy indeed! We get lots of injured and orphaned fledglings (young birds that have just grown their flight feathers) coming in to the centre from about mid-April.

A blackbird that's been attacked by a cat is in one of the cages. Fortunately the wounds were only minor and it will be ready for release in a few days, once the course of antibiotics is complete. It's important to return this bird back to where it was found, because it will have an established territory. I clean out the cage, administer treatment and provide fresh food and water.

9.30am I finish feeding and cleaning the birds and move in to a room where we have some hedgehogs — we take in more than 500 hedgehogs a year.

One of the hedgehogs was brought in after receiving a nasty back wound from a garden strimmer. It's been very lucky and is responding well to treatment. The wound has now completely healed so this hedgehog can be returned to the wild after a final vet check.

11.30am This morning I have a mute swan to release. We know it's a juvenile bird that hatched last year because it still has lots of grey/brown cygnet feathers.

The bird was attacked by another swan after landing on a stretch of water where a breeding pair of swans lives. During the breeding season pairs of swans are fiercely territorial and will attempt to chase off any other swans. They will even chase off their own cygnets from previous years!

This juvenile swan didn't sustain any serious injuries so has only been with us for a short time. Obviously it can't be returned back to where it was found, so I release the bird locally into a flock of about 20 other swans. It joins the others without any fuss, which is great.

2pm One of our animal collection officers brings in four orphaned wood mice rescued from a cat that disturbed their nest. The mice are young but their eyes are open and they have been weaned, so all we need to do is provide them with suitable accommodation and food until they are old enough to be released.

Three of the mice are perfectly healthy but the fourth has an injured leg, presumably caused by the cat. It isn't certain yet whether this mouse will make a full recovery but we're hopeful. All the mice are asleep in the artificial nest we made for them so I carefully put out fresh food and water without disturbing them.

4pm My final job for today is to provide fresh food and water to a heron that an inspector rescued from fishing line. It has fully recovered so can be returned to the wild tomorrow.

Bengal tiger

FACT FILE

● Of the five subspecies of tiger that survive today, the Bengal - or Indian - tiger is thought to be the most common, but there are still only a few thousand left in the wild.

● Bengal tigers live in the forests, scrub, mangroves and grasslands of the Indian subcontinent.

● They can grow up to 3m long and 90cm high to the shoulder, and weigh more than 250kg.

● Tigers usually make a kill about every eight days - hunting more often (every five to six days) if still rearing young. Depending on the size of the meal, it can take several days to pick a carcass clean - they feed for an hour, rest, and then feed for another hour.

● Pregnancy lasts for about 103 days before the female gives birth to a litter of up to seven cubs, though two or three is more common.

● Tigers are most at risk from habitat loss (due to human activity), and poaching for both medicine and their beautiful coats.

FUN & GAMES

ODD ONE OUT

Can you spot the odd one out among these swampy pals?

Cottonmouth
Mudskipper
Green cat-eyed

Mangrove
Pacu
Piranha

Beat that!

Can you dazzle us by finding loads of words of three letters or more from

CROCODILE?

1-15
You must be stuck in the mud – have a look for some more.

16-25
Better, but keep looking. And make it snappy!

We found **50!** Can you beat that?

26-35
Now you're making a bit of a splash. Any more?

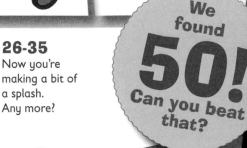

36+
Brilliant! You're as sharp as a croc's teeth!

ANSWERS ON PAGE 94

Pet care

THE RIGHT PET FOR YOU?

Goldfish are brilliant pets to watch in an aquarium or outside in a pond. They may seem a basic pet to look after, but in fact they need a regime of good husbandry, including a suitable diet and regular water maintenance. They can live for over 20 years so goldfish require commitment.

Goldfish

WHAT DO GOLDFISH NEED?

🍽 FOOD AND WATER

- Goldfish eat a well-balanced diet. Special goldfish foods containing all the nutrition your goldfish needs should be fed two to three times a day.
- When kept in a heated aquarium they only need to be fed as much food as they can eat in a few minutes.
- For a treat, you can feed your goldfish live food, such as bloodworms and brine shrimp. Most will also enjoy fresh raw spinach or chopped lettuce.
- Certain plants will give goldfish a bit more food, provide shade, increase the oxygen in the water and add interest. Your vet should be able to tell you which plants you can use.

🏠 A GOOD HOME

- The RSPCA doesn't like goldfish bowls – they are generally far too small for goldfish – preferring aquariums or ponds, although some fancy goldfish are unsuited to outdoor ponds.
- You need to keep any waste in the aquarium to a minimum. You can do this by regularly removing leftover food and faeces, taking dead leaves from plants and removing algae from the aquarium glass.

- The more fish there are in the aquarium, the bigger the aquarium you will need. Generally, goldfish need 60 square centimetres of surface area to every 1cm of fish.
- The water temperature should be between 10 and 25°C.
- Your aquarium should also be fitted with a filter and an aerator. The filter helps keep the water clean and the aerator pumps air through the aquarium, oxygenating the water.

💙 COMPANY

- Goldfish like the company of their own kind so a few friendly fish should be kept together.
- Find out which types of fish can live together if you're thinking of keeping other types of fish with your goldfish.

🐾 TO BEHAVE NORMALLY

- Provide your goldfish with a large enough home, with enough interest to allow normal behaviour.
- Gravel, rocks and plants will allow them to hide and forage for food.
- Provide company and enough interest in the aquarium for them to shelter.

➕ TO BE HEALTHY

- If you are buying new fish make sure you choose healthy stock from someone with a good reputation.

- Introduce new fish to fish you already have with great care. It may be good to keep them separate for a few days to make sure they have not brought any diseases with them.
- If your fish are gasping at the water surface, it may mean there's low oxygen in the water or parasites affecting the gills. Low oxygen can be corrected by gently splashing the surface of the water, or by changing part of the water for fresh. Parasites will have to be dealt with through your vet or a qualified aquarist (fish specialist).
- Make sure an outdoor pond is deep enough for goldfish to survive any extreme changes in temperature – such as when the pond ices over.
- You will need a responsible person to look after your fish when you are on holiday.

Ask your vet for information about your new pet. Visit the local library for books and leaflets on keeping goldfish healthy.

Somerset Secret

Animal Action visits one of the RSPCA's busiest spots – West Hatch Wildlife and Animal Centre near Taunton in Somerset.

WILD ATTACK

Most wild animals brought to the hospital have been involved in a road traffic accident. Here, hospital vet David Couper examines a young fox that has probably been hit by a car. Vets can tell a lot from using a special piece of equipment called an ophthalmoscope to look into, and behind, an animal's eyes.

This fox was not badly injured so he stayed at the wildlife centre until he was well enough to be returned to the wild. Staff returned the fox very close to where it was found, because it might have an established territory nearby.

FEATHERED FRIENDS

There is no shortage of ducklings at West Hatch! Whatever time of year, there are usually several dozen young birds, ranging from mallard ducklings to herring gull chicks and cygnets, being prepared for release.

Young chicks are put under a heat lamp to help them stay warm when they first arrive at the centre. As they grow they are gradually moved to the outside pools.

This young mallard is on an outside pool, waiting to be released back into the wild.

TAKING FLIGHT

The hospital treats about 4,000 wild birds a year — more than one-quarter are fledglings brought in over spring. Many of them would have had a better chance of survival if they had been left alone to learn to fly and continue being fed by the parent birds.

West Hatch has an arrangement with local homeowners who let the centre build aviaries in their gardens. When ready, the young birds are moved to these aviaries where they are fed and cared for by the homeowner for a short time before being released back into the wild.

This bird of prey is called a hobby. It was brought in with an injured wing, possibly after being hit by a car. Birds of prey are released at special sites, often from purpose-built boxes.

CANINE COMPANIONS

People wanting to adopt dogs from West Hatch are interviewed by staff and can see the dogs that are ready for adoption by looking through a catalogue.

Anita Clark, deputy manager of the centre, says: "We don't let the public walk around the kennels any more because it was becoming too upsetting for the dogs. Also, people would fall in love with the dog before knowing the facts and often these animals were returned as unsuitable. These days we get very few returns."

HEDGEHOG HOSPITAL

West Hatch takes in around 280 hedgehogs a year. In late spring and early summer hedgehogs are brought in with lawnmower injuries — hedgehogs hibernate in gardens and can often be injured by lawnmowers and strimmers.

Winter is also a tricky time for some hedgehogs. In fact, in November/December 2007 West Hatch took in 111 hedgehogs. Most of these would have been young hedgehogs, too small to hibernate. It's really important for hedgehogs to eat a lot and lay down enough fat to make it through hibernation over winter.

Pet care

THE RIGHT PET FOR YOU?

If you're interested in keeping reptiles, the RSPCA recommends that you research the care of these creatures very carefully before buying one. Specialist care, including diet, humidity, lighting and the correct temperature, all has to be right. They can be very difficult pets to keep and can live for a very long time.

Reptiles

WHAT DO REPTILES NEED?

🐾 FOOD AND WATER

- All snakes are carnivorous and eat a variety of foods – small mammals, fish, birds, eggs, insects and snails. Your specialist vet will advise you what, and how often, to feed your snake.
- A lizard's diet is varied: some eat mostly insects, while iguanas eat leaves, fruit and flowers. On the other hand, the frilled lizard will eat small mammals and pieces of meat. A specialist keeper or vet will advise you.
- Make sure a bowl of fresh, clean water is provided. Check if a water bowl, spraying a fine mist or a drip system is best for your reptile to drink naturally. Some snakes may even like to swim.

🏠 A GOOD HOME

- Snakes and lizards can vary greatly in size, from less than 1m for many snakes, to up to 10m for a reticulated python. The reptile's environment should reflect the animal's individual needs.
- Conditions must allow them to maintain their body temperature. Reptiles are 'ectothermic', i.e. warmed up by external heat sources, so require a range of temperatures in their vivarium (a large tank that houses reptiles) to do this.
- Your snake or lizard will need access to 'full spectrum' lighting to provide good conditions for growth and development.
- Snakes and lizards need to shed their skin as they grow and to help them do this you need to provide rough surfaces and maintain ventilation and humidity.
- Take care when choosing a floor covering for the vivarium – choose one that allows natural behaviour, like burrowing. Also, make sure that it won't hurt your reptile if it eats it.

♡ COMPANY

- Some snakes and lizards prefer to live alone (for example the common garter snake), while others prefer company. This will depend on the type of snake or lizard you have.

🐾 TO BEHAVE NORMALLY

- In the wild, snakes and lizards like to hide, bathe or stay up in branches, so the home you provide must allow such activities.
- The correct changes in light levels, temperature and humidity will all help your snake or lizard to behave naturally.

➕ TO BE HEALTHY

- Check your snake or lizard every day for illness or injury, and if you suspect it is unwell take it to a specialist vet immediately.
- Regular check-ups by a vet will help prevent any illnesses and keep your snake or lizard in good condition.
- You will need to find a responsible person, who knows about keeping these animals, to look after your snake or lizard when you are on holiday.

Visit your local library or use the internet to find out more information on your specific pet.

Golden eagle

FACT FILE

● The golden eagle is Britain's second largest bird of prey and is seen mainly in Scotland.

● The females are larger than the males, with a wingspan of over 2m!

● Golden eagles prey on rabbits, hares, grouse and even animals as large as lambs.

● An eagle's killing weapons are its talons, which it plunges in to its prey as it swoops down on them from above. Size is not a problem – they can carry the equivalent of five bags of sugar up into the air with them!

● On the west coast of Scotland golden eagles live on sea cliffs.

● The male and female take turns to sit on the eggs in the nest. The female incubates the eggs while her mate hunts, and then he takes over while she goes to find food for herself.

● There are currently just over 440 breeding pairs in Britain.

Pet Care

THE RIGHT PET FOR YOU?

Visit your local library or use the internet to find out more information on your specific pet.

Small mammals make interesting pets, but each has its own specific needs.

Small furries

GUINEA PIGS

THE RIGHT PET FOR YOU?

Guinea pigs are friendly and easily tamed, but they need commitment and regular attention. Long-haired guinea pigs can be especially difficult to look after. They also need large homes that can be expensive to create. These pets can live for four to eight years so caring for a guinea pig is a big responsibility.

WHAT DO GUINEA PIGS NEED?

FOOD AND WATER

- Guinea pigs are grazing animals and need a balanced and interesting diet to be happy and healthy.
- Most of their diet is made up of hay, but they should also have cereals, green leafy vegetables and carrot tops, and fruit such as pear, apple and melon.
- A constant supply of fresh, clean drinking water, preferably in a drip feed bottle with a metal spout, needs to be provided.
- Guinea pigs can suffer from vitamin C deficiency. Symptoms include lameness, an altered shuffling gait, swollen joints, a rough coat and depression. Ask your vet for advice on how to provide your pets with an adequate supply of this vitamin.

A GOOD HOME

- Guinea pigs need a large, spacious enclosure with a big shelter for sleeping and resting, a toilet area, a feeding area and lots of room to exercise.
- They also need places to hide if they feel frightened. These 'refuges' should have at least two exits to prevent dominant guinea pigs becoming aggressive to other guinea pigs inside them. There should be as many refuges are there are guinea pigs, plus one more. Cardboard boxes with two cut-out exits or large fired-clay pipes make good refuges.
- Provide your guinea pigs with appropriate bedding to keep them warm and comfortable.

- The toilet area must be cleaned every day and wet or soiled materials replaced with clean ones. The shelter will also need a full clean every week.
- Any home must be safe from predators and provide protection from draughts, direct sunlight and very hot or cold weather.

COMPANY

- Guinea pigs are sociable and need to be with other friendly guinea pigs, unless there is a good welfare reason not to. A guinea pig made to live alone may suffer.
- Try to choose littermates of the same sex – although you should never keep more than two male guinea pigs (over four months old) together.
- Guinea pigs need to be able to avoid contact with humans or other guinea pigs if they want to. Refuges can allow them to hide.
- The widespread practice of keeping guinea pigs and rabbits together is not recommended because they require different diets, they often fight and they spread diseases to each other.
- Your guinea pigs need to be looked after by a responsible person when you are on holiday.

TO BEHAVE NORMALLY

- Guinea pigs need exercise every day in a secure enclosure, which is preferably

attached to their main shelter, so they can come and go as they please.
- Guinea pigs are grazing animals so scattering some of their food for them to find will give them something to do and reflect a natural behaviour. Providing appropriate objects to gnaw, such as untreated apple wood, is also important to keep your guinea pig's teeth healthy.

TO BE HEALTHY

- Check your guinea pig for signs of injury or illness every day, and take it to a vet for regular health checks and advice. If you suspect your guinea pig is poorly, ask an adult to take it to a vet immediately.
- Carefully groom your guinea pig regularly (ask your vet to show you how to brush your guinea pig the right way), especially if it is a long-haired breed.

HAMSTERS

THE RIGHT PET FOR YOU?

Hamsters are lively and clean, and most prefer to live alone, although some dwarf species will live in pairs. They can take time to become tame and need to have peace and quiet during the day because they're nocturnal. Hamsters are difficult to look after well and need lots of space and an interesting environment in which to live. Depending on the species, they can live for up to three years.

WHAT DO HAMSTERS NEED?

🥫 FOOD AND WATER

- Hamsters eat a food mix, which contains mostly cereal and grains. But they can also be fed small amounts of seeds, peanuts, carrots, root vegetables and pieces of apple.
- In the wild, hamsters are omnivorous (meaning they eat meat and vegetables) and they hoard food. You can encourage hunting for food and hoarding by scattering some of your hamster's food on its bedding.
- A constant supply of fresh, clean drinking water in a drip feed bottle with a metal spout should be provided.

🏠 A GOOD HOME

- A hamster's housing should be as large and as interesting as possible. It should be located out of direct sunlight, have a solid base and, because hamsters are burrowing animals, have a deep layer of appropriate bedding on the floor.
- Hamsters need a nest box in which to hide and sleep as well as store food. Hay and plain paper (such as kitchen roll) should be provided as nesting material.
- A cage should never be a hamster's only home. Your hamster should be allowed to regularly exercise outside the cage. This should always be supervised and in a safe and secure area.
- Providing different kinds of tubes in its housing will encourage your hamster to explore, as well as give it somewhere to hide.
- It's important to clean a hamster's house regularly, but changing the bedding and nesting material can be very stressful for the hamster, so keep a bit of the old familiar-smelling nest material every time.

💙 COMPANY

- Apart from some dwarf species, hamsters prefer to live alone.
- A responsible person should look after your hamster when you are away on holiday.

🐾 TO BEHAVE NORMALLY

- Hamsters are very active and need to exercise in a large, secure enclosure every day.
- Hamsters are nocturnal (this means they sleep during the day) and should not be disturbed when they are resting, or they may become distressed.
- Hamsters should be encouraged to hunt for food and store it wherever they choose.
- Providing appropriate objects to gnaw, such as untreated apple wood, is also important to keep your hamster's teeth healthy.
- Hamsters should be provided with places to hide when they are frightened.

✚ TO BE HEALTHY

- Check your hamster for signs of injury or illness every day, and take it to a vet for regular health checks and advice. If you suspect your hamster is poorly, ask an adult to take it to a vet immediately.
- Hamsters with long hair should be carefully groomed regularly.

RATS

THE RIGHT PET FOR YOU?

Rats are intelligent, interesting pets but need a lot of space and attention. Rats live for up to three-and-a-half years so need a lot of time and commitment.

WHAT DO RATS NEED?

🥫 FOOD AND WATER

- A balanced healthy commercial rat diet is ideal, plus some fruit and vegetables for a treat.
- They also need a constant supply of fresh, clean drinking water in a drip feed bottle with a metal spout.

🏠 A GOOD HOME

- Rats need a large enclosure on more than one level, with plenty of hiding places so they can explore and not become bored.
- The enclosure must be kept in a warm place indoors, out of direct sunlight.
- There must be a nest box and other hiding places inside their home, with two exits so that a rat can escape any dominant intruder. If you have two rats, you should provide at least three hiding places.
- Rats need appropriate bedding to keep warm, dry and comfortable.
- It's important to clean your rats' enclosure regularly, but changing the bedding and nesting material can be very stressful for the animal, so keep a bit of the old familiar-smelling nest material every time. It should be thoroughly cleaned every week.

💙 COMPANY

- Rats are extremely sociable and should be kept with at least one other rat. They should also have human company for at least part of the day.
- A responsible person should look after your rats when you are on holiday.

🐾 TO BEHAVE NORMALLY

- Rats are very intelligent creatures and need to explore, so exercise and human company are really important.
- Rats' teeth grow all the time so a non-toxic gnawing block should be provided.
- Toys such as cardboard tubes and non-toxic balls will help entertain rats.

✚ TO BE HEALTHY

- Have your rat neutered to prevent unwanted litters.
- Rats should be taken to a vet for regular check-ups, as well as if they become ill or are injured.

GERBILS

THE RIGHT PET FOR YOU?

Gerbils are bright, inquisitive and fun to observe, but they need your commitment and regular attention as well as a large and interesting home. They will live for three to four years.

WHAT DO GERBILS NEED?

🐾 FOOD AND WATER

- Feed your gerbil daily on a diet of mixed grain and some washed fruit and vegetables, with a few sunflower seeds (although you must not give them too many of these) and peanuts.
- Provide a constant supply of fresh, clean drinking water in a drip feed bottle with a metal spout.

🏠 A GOOD HOME

- Gerbils need a large home called a gerbilarium (like a big aquarium tank with a wire mesh cover) that's kept indoors in a warm place, out of direct sunlight.
- Gerbils need to burrow so they must have plenty of appropriate burrowing material as well as suitable bedding.
- The gerbilarium must be thoroughly cleaned out every week. It's important to clean a gerbil's house regularly, but changing the bedding and nesting material can be very stressful for the animal, so keep a bit of the old familiar-smelling nest material every time.

💚 COMPANY

- Gerbils must be kept with other friendly gerbils, but make sure they're all of the same sex to prevent breeding.

- Gerbils need to be looked after by a responsible person when you are away on holiday.

🐾 TO BEHAVE NORMALLY

- Gerbils are very active and need to burrow, scratch and dig, so their housing needs to cater for this.
- They are active by day and night, so they need to be given some quiet time to rest.
- Providing toys to play with and gnaw will give gerbils something interesting to do. Suitable toys include cardboard tubes, egg boxes, untreated apple wood, and non-toxic, untreated wooden cotton reels.

➕ TO BE HEALTHY

- Check your gerbil for signs of injury or illness every day, and take it to a vet for regular health checks and advice. If you suspect your gerbil is poorly, ask an adult to take it to a vet immediately.

FERRETS

THE RIGHT PET FOR YOU?

Ferrets are lively, playful and easily tamed, but they need a lot of space. They can bite (hard!) and emit a strong musky smell. They live between eight and 10 years so you must be committed to looking after this pet for a long time.

WHAT DO FERRETS NEED?

🐾 FOOD AND WATER

- Ferrets are carnivores and need to eat a balanced meat-based diet to stay healthy. Commercial ferret biscuits are now available.
- A constant supply of fresh, clean drinking water in a drip feed bottle with a metal spout must be provided.

🏠 A GOOD HOME

- Ferrets need a large, weatherproof, secure enclosure to live in. The enclosure must include a shelter to sleep in, a toilet area, a feeding area and a large, interesting area to exercise and play.
- The exercise area should ideally be your house or garden, as ferrets need lots of space. It should be filled with interesting toys for your ferrets to play with as they very quickly become bored.
- They are great escape artists and they like to dig and burrow, so be sure to make absolutely certain your ferret enclosure is escape-proof!

MICE

Mice are lively and easily tamed, but are active at night and may smell (especially males). They live for up to two-and-a-half years so time and commitment is essential.

WHAT DO MICE NEED?

- Provide your ferrets with appropriate bedding to keep them clean and comfortable. It's important to clean your ferrets' enclosure regularly, but changing the bedding and nesting material can be very stressful for the animals, so keep a bit of the old familiar-smelling nest material every time. It should be thoroughly cleaned every week.

COMPANY

- Ferrets should be kept with other friendly ferrets and have human company. Ferrets that are kept together must be neutered to prevent breeding.
- Ferrets can be complicated to keep so it's important to find a suitable person to look after your pets when you are away.

TO BEHAVE NORMALLY

- Ferrets sleep a lot and need to be left to do so.
- Daily exercise and play are vital for ferrets, so provide them with a large area with lots of interesting things to explore, such as cardboard tubes, paper bags and lengths of drainpipe.
- Playtime for ferrets can often be frantic, so it's a good idea to supervise them when they're playing.

TO BE HEALTHY

- It's important to handle ferrets regularly to keep them tame and to check for signs of injury or illness.
- Ferrets can suffer from various diseases, including canine distemper, so take your pet to a vet for regular check-ups and advice, as well as if it becomes ill or injured.
- They can catch flu from you too, so stay away from them if you feel flu coming on.

FOOD AND WATER

- A healthy balanced diet of commercial mouse food (mixed grains) with some washed fruit and vegetables is ideal.
- A constant supply of fresh, clean drinking water in a drip feed bottle with a metal spout must be available.

A GOOD HOME

- Mice should have a large enclosure on more than one level, with plenty of toys, such as cardboard tubes.
- It should be positioned in a warm place indoors, out of direct sunlight.
- You must provide a nest box inside their home, with two exits to enable a mouse to escape from any dominant mouse.
- The enclosure must have plenty of hiding places (each preferably with two exits). If you have four mice, for example, you must provide five hiding places.
- Mice must be provided with appropriate bedding material to keep them warm, dry and comfortable.
- It's important to clean your mouse enclosure regularly, but changing the bedding and nesting material can be very stressful for the animals, so keep a bit of the old familiar-smelling nest material every time. It should be thoroughly cleaned every week.

COMPANY

- Mice are very sociable animals and should not be kept alone; they must be with other mice.
- A pair of females is easiest, although larger groups of females usually get on well. Groups of male mice tend to fight. Also, keeping males and females apart will avoid unwanted litters.
- A responsible person must look after your mice when you are on holiday.

TO BEHAVE NORMALLY

- Mice are nocturnal, so are active during the evening and in the night. They must be allowed to sleep during the day.
- A mouse's teeth grow all the time so provide a gnawing block to keep teeth short and healthy.

TO BE HEALTHY

- Take your mice to a vet for regular check-ups, as well as if they are ill or injured.

RSPCA

ANIMAL
Action

WATER VOLE

ANIMAL Action

BLACK AND WHITE RUFFED LEMUR

Animal magic

Can you turn a calf into a foal? By changing one letter to make a new word, you can! Use the clues to help you.

CALF

.... Shout out or telephone someone

.... Topple off something or collapse on the floor

.... When you don't pass a test

.... Very thin metal used in cooking

FOAL

WORDSEARCH

Spring has sprung and all around baby animals are being born!
Can you find the 12 spring babies in the grid? They may appear forwards, backwards, up, down or diagonally.

- CALF
- CHICK
- CYGNET
- DUCKLING
- FAWN
- FOAL
- GOSLING
- KID
- KITTEN
- LAMB
- PIGLET
- PUPPY

```
I P S L K A E F C A L F
K I D D P D E H T A Y E
D G E T E U I E H G A L
L L S I O C P R H N T M
A E O M K K J P O I T F
M T R O R L H F Y L E L
B H T O H I B W L S A R
K I T T E N H O C O N S
N I R H E G A O F G E O
B S Y I T I R E R A T E
T C Y G N E T S U R W C
G L F H A O E S A T N N
```

Ben's World

IT SAYS HERE, BEN, THAT IF YOU TALK TO A PLANT IT WILL RESPOND.

© MIKE ORAM & JOHN PICKERING

APPARENTLY THEY ARE VERY SENSITIVE TO OUR THOUGHTS!

BEFORE YOU SAY ANYTHING, GORDON, I **DID** SAY PLEASE!

GAMES

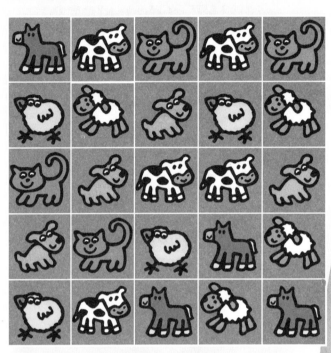

SPOT THE EXTRA

Have a good look at the grid. Six baby animals are shown. Five of them appear four times, but one appears five times – which one?

Linkwords

Can you find the animals that link the first word to the second?

E.g. rocking......horse........chestnut

spring ....wool

hush ....love

pussy...nip

fox ....scout

Which is the odd one out and why?

Beat that!

Baby ducks can be very cute, but how many words of three letters or more can you make from the word

DUCKLING?

Up to 10
Sounds like you haven't even hatched yet! Come on, keep looking – it's not that hard!

11-15
That's a bit better – now waddle off and find some more.

16-20
Now you're in the swim. Keep looking.

21-25
Brilliant! You've really spread your wings. Can you go for the top spot?

We found just **29!** Can you beat that?

26+
Truly amazing! That was so hard it must have driven you quackers!

ANSWERS ON PAGE 94

Wicked

Enjoy these spooky spun treats. but don't worry about the spiders - they moved out ages ago!

WHAT YOU NEED

- Ready-made plain sponge cakes
- 200g icing sugar
- Mixing bowl
- Warm water
- Wooden spoon
- Round-ended knife
- Teaspoon chocolate powder
- Ready-made icing in tubes
- Cocktail stick

You can buy plain, un-iced sponge cakes from supermarkets, or make your own using a pack of cake mix!

webs!

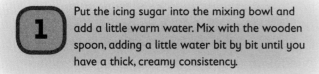

1 Put the icing sugar into the mixing bowl and add a little warm water. Mix with the wooden spoon, adding a little water bit by bit until you have a thick, creamy consistency.

2 Use the knife to spread the white icing over half of the cup cakes. Leave to one side. Add the chocolate powder to the rest of the icing. Mix well and use to ice the rest of the cakes.

3 When the icing is dry, squeeze the ready-made tube icing in circles, starting with a small circle in the middle and making the circles bigger towards the outside edge.

4 Before the icing has had a chance to harden, take the cocktail stick and carefully drag straight lines from the middle to the outside edge. This creates the spider's-web effect!

FUN & GAMES
Answers

9
Whooooo's missing? –
the waving owl.

Odd one out – tortoise (it's a
reptile, the rest are mammals).

19
Pondlife – legs = freshwater
shrimp, water boatman,
water mite, dragonfly.
no legs = pea-shell cockle,
swan mussel, pond snail,
ramshorn snail.

21
Riddle of the swamp – mosquito.

28–29
Odd one out – Colours: cob
(it's a breed). Markings: sock
(it's a leg marking, the rest
are face markings). Tack: bit
(it's a part of a bridle, the
rest are parts of the saddle.)
Food: shavings (they're used
for bedding, the rest are foods).
Feet: poll (it's part of the
head, the rest are on the feet).

Top and tail trail – Trot, tail, leg,
gallop, ponies, saddle, Exmoor,
roan, numnah, haynet.

Pony puzzler – Shetland.

75
Odd one out – mudskipper (it's a
fish, the other two are types of
snake) and mangrove (it's a type
of tree, the others are fish).

90–91
Linkwords – lambs, puppy, cat,
cub. Cat is the odd one out as
all the others are names of
young or baby animals.

Animal magic – CALF, call, fall,
fail, foil, FOAL.

Spot the extra – calf.

HOW DID YOU DO?

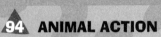

PICTURE CREDITS

RSPCA

IDEAL IF YOU ARE AGED BETWEEN 7 AND 12!

CHECK OUT: www.rspca.org.uk/under8teenz

Love animals?

Join the Animal Action Club!

Get a fab **FREE** pack and **SEVEN** issues of the magazine delivered to your door **ALL FOR ONLY £11!***

(MORE THAN 20% OFF SHOP PRICE)

Your pack includes: a calendar; puzzle book; badge and your own membership card.

SUBSCRIBE TO *ANIMAL ACTION* MAGAZINE AND BECOME A MEMBER OF THE ANIMAL ACTION CLUB

Every issue is **jam-packed** with animal fun including:

- Real life rescues
- Fun & games
- Pets pix
- Drawing tips
- Fab posters

GET A GREAT FREE GIFT WITH YOUR FIRST MAGAZINE!

RSPCA, Wilberforce Way, Southwater, Horsham, West Sussex RH13 9RS Telephone: 0300 123 0100 A charity registered in England and Wales, no: 219099
ILLUSTRATIONS: SONIA CANALS.

Three easy ways to join!

Ask an adult to:

1. Send your name, address and date of birth along with a cheque or postal order (made payable to the RSPCA) to: **Animal Action Club, RSPCA, Wilberforce Way, Southwater, Horsham, West Sussex RH13 9RS.**

2. Call: **0300 123 0346** and pay by debit/credit card.

3. Go to: **www.rspca.org.uk/under8teenz** and click on *Join us* under the Animal Action Club section.

Please quote **AAANN08** when joining.